THE FOGG[...]DIA

THE FOGGIEST IDEA

❀

Tales of a Displaced Texan in San Francisco Mamaland

Robin Dutton-Cookston

iUniverse, Inc.
New York   Bloomington

The Foggiest Idea

Tales of a Displaced Texan in San Francisco Mamaland

iUniverse books may be ordered through booksellers or by contacting:

iUniverse
1663 Liberty Drive
Bloomington, IN 47403
www.iuniverse.com
1-800-Authors (1-800-288-4677)

ISBN: 978-1-4401-0376-6(pbk)
ISBN: 978-1-4401-0377-3 (ebk)

Printed in the United States of America

iUniverse rev. date 11/03/08

For Jeff
And Grace
And for Rosemary, who is already inspiring the next book.

Table of Contents

Foreward
by Karrie McAllister

A famous person once said, "Being a mother is the second hardest job in the world. The first hardest is, of course, having to screen endless episodes of *Teletubbies*."

OK, that person isn't so famous. It's me. But come on, we all know it's God's honest truth that being a mother is hard work, almost as much as we know how much the *Teletubbies* suck. (No offense to any Tinky Winky fans, if you even exist.)

But saying that motherhood is hard is pretty clichéd. Every mother knows it, most fathers admit it when they have to, and non-parents roll their eyes because they've never actually felt what it's like to go four years without a solid night of sleep or have cracked nipples. They don't know what it's like to watch your oldest child disappear onto a school bus for the first time. They just don't know because they just can't comprehend how much a mother can love her child.

It's scary, really.

There is nothing in the world that a mom could want more than to give her children everything in the entire world, in total perfection. We want the best for our kids. The best health, the best education, the best principles, the best emotions. We want them to have it all, or at the very least, more than we had. And because of this dire need to fulfill every wish and fantasy so that they'll not spend their 20's and 30's on the couch of some psychologist saying, "man, my childhood was totally screwed up," we literally bust our asses day in and day out (seriously—I've got scars that may or may not be stretchmarks) over-exerting ourselves to the point of pain and doing our best not to make any major mistakes.

I offer up this little anecdote which can best summarize my philosophy on motherhood. I like to call it "The Popcorn Incident," although that's not a very catchy title.

It all started on a fall afternoon, when I was grossly pregnant with my third child. And because the veins in my legs had had just about enough of this pregnancy crap, they gave out and I was required by doc to wear full length compression hose which I mention only because they made me flammable from head to toe. I was attempting to race (read: waddle) around the house, trying to achieve some order and neatness so that the playgroup friends who would be over in a short while to celebrate my son's birthday wouldn't think I had totally given up on cleanliness. But I also had to pick up my oldest daughter from school. All at the same time.

At this point you may ask yourself, "Why would she plan things so close together? Why wouldn't she give herself some more time?" Let me tell you, the thought crossed my mind. But in order for everyone to be happy (read: except me), this is what had to be done.

And I also had to make "sweetie popcorn," my son's favorite snack, for the gathering. So there, belly bulging, I poured the oil, sugar, salt, and popcorn kernels into the pot. I cranked up the stove and began the popping process. When it came time to start shaking the pot so that the bottom kernels didn't turn into a black burnt mess, I grabbed some potholders to protect my hands.

To make a short story long, I caught one of the potholders on fire so I had to run it to the sink which meant that I was creating that black burnt mess in the pot. So I ran back to the stove, turned it off, and whipped the lid off the pot to cool down the contents and stop the cooking process.

And then a sticky kernel shot right out and burnt a big red dot into my forehead, just above my right eyebrow. Somehow I managed to thank the lord that I hadn't caught my entire body on fire, raced out the door to pick up my eldest child, and back home just in time greet my playdate friends. While the kids played, I had to explain to them why I looked the way I did and why I was telling them to eat the damn popcorn because I lost valuable skin (and a potholder) for my son's special snack.

And they laughed, because they UNDERSTOOD.

They understood why I did the things I did, because they do them too. We're all just a bunch of nuts, but nuts that go together, bound by our maternal job description.

When I first read Robin Dutton-Cookston I knew instantly that we connected on some cosmic level that included giggling about fruit snacks and baby slings. And even though she's raising her kids in the ultra-hip metropolis of San Francisco and I am raising mine in an ultra-Amish metropolis of northern Ohio, we still connect, which is why I love listening to her stories and that life on the other side of the buggy trail is still just that—life.

We're women, we're mothers. We stick together like caramelized popcorn to forehead skin because in understanding each other's stories, we become better mothers. That's why we need to hear the tales of other mommies' mishaps and story-time struggles. We need to hear that we're not the first to watch a baby fall off the bed, and we need to hear that if it happens, baby will be OK. We need to see that we're not the only one in the world going gray over where to send our kids to preschool. We need to know, even in our weakest moments, that we do what we do because we love our kids and that most importantly, we are not alone in this, the second hardest job in the world.

Long live Tinky Winky.

-Karrie McAllister, Author of *Small Town Soup: Good for What Ails You*

Preface

What's it like to go from sitting two rows behind George W. Bush in church to explaining ass-less chaps to a two-year-old while wandering through the Castro neighborhood of San Francisco? Or how about learning to handle a contact high with my child at a Mission Street bus stop while nostalgic for a Texas truckstop waitress who calls me "Sugar?"

We moved to San Francisco already pregnant, only I didn't know it until after the first week in my new city. I peed on the stick and discovered I was expecting while still unpacking boxes shortly after my husband and I plunked down into our charming Victorian apartment on Alamo Square. (Alamo Square Park faces the row of houses you always see in the credits for *Full House*—a famous San Francisco landmark.) I quickly unearthed the universal trappings of motherhood while still learning to navigate the many complicated layers of my adopted city. And I found myself in a forced enrollment into the never-ending school of urban parenting, where city living with small children offers many teachable moments regarding public transportation, gender-bending individuals, and the homeless.

As a displaced, albeit liberal-leaning, Texas native, always honing my transplant-parenting skills out here in San Francisco, I started writing about my family's experiences when my first daughter was still a baby. I quickly realized that even the most mundane and commonplace parenting mishaps took on a unique edge under the glittering eye of San Francisco, one of our nation's most beloved and progressive cities.

The book that follows chronicles those universal rites of passage that all new moms have in common, as well as all the times I pondered on the incomparable experience of raising a child in San Francisco, where rent costs more than the gross national product of some small countries, and people who have kids are looked down upon as "breeders" among certain circles. What you have before you is a collection of essays that offers an insider's take on San Francisco parenthood through the eyes of a former small-town Texas gal, uprooted from conservative oil and soil and thrust into the most liberal city in America. As you peruse these foggy ideas you may not unearth nuggets of wisdom in every paragraph, but I hope you will at least find something you can relate to, and maybe have a chuckle or two.

Happy Reading!

She Bang! She Bang!

My child is a headbanger. Although still a baby, my fourteen-month old busts a move that rivals a Motley Crue audience member, circa 1986. On numerous occasions throughout the day, she thrashes her head back and forth, Metallica-style, knocking both the front and back of her cranium into various hard and soft surfaces. This disturbs me.

Grace doesn't go heavy metal out of anger or frustration. Her animated, and I imagine often painful, head butts are part of her lively play routine, alongside stomping, clapping, bouncing, and an organic free-form breakdancing bit that we like to call "quickie feet." However, these other antics don't have the immediate possibility of a concussion, unless she slips while doing a baby version of the Robot and takes a dance-time wipeout. Headbanging, depending on Grace's surface du jour, poses a much greater threat of bodily harm. Thank God for those thick-as-a-brick baby skulls and extra layers of head cushioning.

The preferred surface for her hourly Headbangers Ball varies according to Grace's mood, the time of day, and the level of parental interference. Mellow, post-breakfast mornings create a groovy scene for crashin' her noggin onto the sleeping cat, while pre-bedtime energy bursts just scream "Daddy! Bring me your forehead so I can hurtle my skull into yours!"

Other enjoyable victims include but are not limited to: sofa pillows, walls, linoleum, the side of the bathtub, the oven door, windowpanes, doorknobs, and guitars. While each of these surfaces provide their own unique tactile experiences and accompanying percussive beats, by far the most annoying head crashing comes at 6:00 a.m. Grace decides to wake Mama for her morning nurse at this time by jamming her frontal lobe into whichever body part is most accessible. Sometimes the shoulder, sometimes the cheek, sometimes the boob. Sometimes Mama bruises.

Last week, we had one of those days where the house seemed to explode from within. Wooden blocks, piles of onesies, plastic cups, and cracker crumbs littered the living room to the height of Grace's shoulders, creating a challenging obstacle course for both of us. In anticipation of Daddy coming home and re-igniting the debate over whether our sparkling-clean dwelling is in truth Mama's well-fed illusion, I decided to bulldoze the crap into the corner behind the entertainment center, my secret quick clean hideaway. While I distractedly shoveled a path through the plastic debris field, I turned my back on Grace, who was happily shredding Daddy's comic books by the fireplace.

A dull thud suddenly echoed behind me, followed by a familiar screech. I turned around from my hurried toy hiding to see Grace smack her head hard on the fireplace for a second time. Apparently, one brick bash was not enough for my budding masochist. Grace rolled off of her fireplace perch and plopped her diapered hiney on the hardwoods with a more muffled thud. She rubbed her reddening forehead and wailed.

"Grace! Why do you do that, you goofball?" I rhetorically cooed as I scooped her up for a little boo-boo sugar. Planting a smooch on her inflamed forehead, I whispered, "You are such a silly little headknocker." She snorted appreciatively, and I hoped my pet name didn't sound like an encouragement. Grace has not attempted the fireplace bang since that day, but I have seen her eyeing the flagstones in the back garden with a curiously practiced head nod.

Based on the spastic energy levels of both my husband and myself, I knew that I had the potential to create quite a wiggly child. I anticipated a baby who could match Daddy's frenzied armpit tickle sessions and keep up with Mama's inability to sit still for longer than ten minutes without sedation. As a woman who physically cannot stop pacing the living room when talking on the phone, I knew that I would empathize with an intensely energetic child. But Grace's head knocking really caught me off guard, bringing our family activity level to a whole new Emergency Room plane. Sometimes I wondered, if she headbangs now, what will it be when she is five, full body moshing?

I have heard that professional ice skaters often build their careers around one intricate, loopedy-loop, heart-stopping twirl that becomes the signature piece of their performance. Similarly, we all know how the world's most talented musicians, either by chance or skill, often create one climactic song that becomes integral to a band's very identity. In the vast repertoire of Grace's headbanging, the Shoe-Tie-Head-Crash is Grace's "Stairway To Heaven."

With the same predictability of George W. Bush's vacation schedule, Grace and I endure this daily thrusting each time we go through the routine of tying her Big Girl shoes. Grace sits on my lap, with her back to my torso, while I nervously try to beat the clock before the banging begins, knowing full well that I will fail. With a thrash that has been honed with the precision dedication of an Olympic gymnast, Grace begins to jerk her head violently back and forth, just as I finish the double knot on shoe one.

I am now forced to duck and dodge the incoming head missiles lest I take one to the chin, cheek, or sternum. The baby whiplash continues until the all laces are knotted in such a way that they will not come undone unless I pick at them for an hour or else Grace discovers scissors. This ensures that I only have to do the shoe-tie defensive play once daily. The entire event takes up to ten minutes, not a long time in the non-baby world, but an eternity when forced to simultaneously dress and dodge a hyperactive little ram.

Grace's attempts to crack her own head open remind me of the biggest lesson I have, so far, obtained from Mamahood: letting go of control. My new identity continually offers opportunities for this impatient, control-freak mama to stop trying so hard to manage Grace's behavior and let her be her own person. In these situations, where I wish Grace's wardrobe included a football helmet, I try to strike a balance between allowing Grace to celebrate her energy and stopping her from knocking herself out. It is a constant struggle, where I find myself laughing at her repeated giggly head butts to the teddy bear and, in the next minute, lunging like a rugby player to stop her from putting her head through a department store window. Until I get the balance right, I will continue to turn to the Quiet Riot tape I fished out of my sixth grade keepsake box. It reminds me that my family is not alone in our headbanging world.

Bang your head! Metal health will drive you mad!

The Best Reality Show Ever

Sometimes I wonder why I get so puritanical about what deviance my daughter, Grace, might accidentally see on TV. Especially since Miami-style vice seems to lurk around every corner of San Francisco. Why do I worry about scripted sleaze when a jaunt to the Civic Center farmer's market offers a guided tour of the Seven Deadly Sins? The Tube has got nothing on my adopted City when it comes to giving my baby an eye-opening glimpse of the wacky world of, well, humans. But for some reason, I can't get too jacked up about it.

For example, today I may have caught a secondhand buzz from a spliff-smoking madman. (Note to those who did not attend a liberal arts university or have only recently moved to San Francisco: spliff = marijuana.)

At first I didn't realize who had the bud, as I was distracted by Grace's demands to sing round after round of *Itsy Bitsy Spider* during our wait for the #48 bus at the corner of 24th and Mission. Considering the neighborhood, the waves of ganja smoke could have emanated from the pair of hipsters in vintage-style T-shirts, the woman in the purple fez who hid under a bench, or any number of young men wearing athletic jerseys and what looked like black pantyhose on their heads.

I edged away from a surly mustachioed teenager, my perceived source of stink, by dancing my backpack-contained-tot further under the protective awning of the bus stop. The weed smell stayed with me. Finally, a man with Coke-bottle glasses and long, disheveled hair jumped up from the bench under the bus stop shelter.

"Have a seat, mama!" he warbled, not unlike Tommy Chong—of the legendary pot movie duo, Cheech and Chong.

"No, thank you," I half smiled and looked away, not wanting to encourage any blossoming friendships.

"Hey, I was gonna move anyway, because I'm smokin' my weed and you shouldn't do that around kids, you know?"

He ambled into the street, narrowly missing a pimped-out Cadillac, and disappeared into the McDonalds for, no doubt, some McNuggets to satisfy his munchies. I glanced back at Grace, whose interest in a mural of the Virgin Mary was too rapt to be soiled by interactions with the Stoner Man, shrugged it off, and got on the bus.

This incident got me to thinking about what a weenie I am to fret over Grace tumbling about the living room while my husband watches football, a.k.a. the neofascist cryptic metaphor for nuclear war. (Many thanks to Robert Downey, Jr.'s character from the Rodney Dangerfield classic, *Back to School,* for that gem.)

It's not just gladiator, man-punching sports that give me Protective Mama jeebs. It's adult television in general. When I found out that Grace discovered the "on" button for the Brain Rotter all by herself, I broke out in a cold sweat, fearing that one day she might stumble across frightfully inappropriate primetime fare: an especially nauseating episode of *Fear Factor,* a confusing sex-riddled rerun of *Dawson's Creek* or, God forbid such evil, a Janet Jackson booby.

This televised swill alarms me more than the grand funk reality show we see daily in San Francisco, antics that, for better or worse, never sidled up to the manicured lawns and station wagons of my West Texas childhood.

Read on for more sights my wee one has seen (of course, you are probably aware that this is the more printable stuff):

Naked men wearing gorilla masks in a footrace. Grace saw her first "Bay to Breakers" race, from the sidelines, when she was about three months old, too little to laugh at the costumed squad of 20-somethings who drunkenly struggled to push a keg on a skateboard up the Hayes Street hill. She was also blissfully unaware of the nude simians jiggling along without their jock straps. But don't think Mama didn't notice.

Facially pierced street kids in Haight-Ashbury. Back when my generation's old-fogy parents grew their sideburns long and found transcendence with a Jefferson Airplane LP, this neighborhood served as hippie headquarters. Nowadays, I love it for awesome thrift-store shopping and intense-looking body modifications. Beauty is in the eye of the beholder, but I am still squeamish enough to shrink away from those who find beauty in the stud stuck through the eyelid.

Gavin Newsom's hair. Okay, I know we're getting silly, but there is something unnatural about the crest of the wave on our mayor's coif. I think it's fantastic that he allowed same-sex couples to get hitched, and I hope that our daughter will someday see him as a human rights hero. But I still shudder at his gravity defying 'do.

Pretty scary stuff, huh? So why don't I worry? Precisely because these bits and pieces of urban life are the real deal—with the exception of whatever shellac Mayor Gavin coats on that sexy mane. San Franciscans can be confused and weirdly inappropriate, and, just like that mayoral hair, kinda messed up

We make bizarre fashion choices. We meld metal studs with body parts, creating groundbreaking combos that won't hit the Midwest for five more years. But we also help each other out. We tell our friends when we unearth a top secret parking oasis in North Beach. We try not to share our secondhand pot smoke—unless we are at a Dave Matthews concert, where fans appreciate such sharing. We giggle at the schmo in the mask who shows his schlong.

Sure, this once-sheltered country gal sometimes gets a tad freaked when eyeballing a billboard with a cartoon penis that reminds me to get tested for syphilis. But it is a darn good reinforcement that reality works a little differently from a show on Fox, where blood flies and people screw one another with impunity. I hope that by shunning TV and bravely venturing out to be a tiny part of this City's swarm, I can model tolerance and acceptance for my budding open-minded wee one.

At least that's the way I hope it goes. For all I know, I may see her someday in the *San Francisco Chronicle* as the winner of the Bay to Breakers race—wearing nothing but a gorilla mask.

Don't Box Me In, aka Geeks R Us

There are two kinds of people in this world: those who put people into categories of two, and those who don't. Right now I am too buzzed on ancient Halloween candy to remember who uttered that "whoa, dude" bit of wisdom—but I know that it is probably blowing your mind like a Pink Floyd album or a Bill and Ted adventure movie.

I must confess that I fall into the first group. As a card-carrying postmodern feminist, I'm not proud of this. Who am I to stuff people into tightly defined boxes? Such judgment goes against the bleeding heart open-mindedness I am supposed to exude now that I am a San Franciscan. Forcing people into faux classifications also toys with my delicate self-esteem.

Take for instance this shrewd mama-venting blog I read the other day. (Note to my Nana: a blog is an online diary sort of thing.) The author argued in favor of the inherent superiority of a Rocker Mom over a Soccer Mom, with the former being all things hip and awesome, despite the presence of a small parasitic person who demands all things plastic and sugar. Soccer Moms were lambasted as sadly square and pathetic, relics so out-of-date, they may as well be wearing flannel and listening to Pearl Jam.

As any good self-absorbed, modern woman does, I thought about how these labels apply to me.

A Rocker Mom gets tattooed, plays base guitar, and dresses her baby in a leather jacket that says, "Smash the State" above a skull and crossbones. Is this like me? No. No. No.

A Soccer Mom drives a gargantuan SUV, wears matchy-matchy sweater sets, and is on the board of her local Junior League. Again, is this me? Afraid not.

As much as I secretly long to don my tenth-grade denim jacket with the Sex Pistols patch and proudly proclaim myself a Rocker Mom, the sad truth is that I lack a certain, how shall I say, coolness. I know that I would reveal myself as a poseur within ten minutes of trying to infiltrate the Rocker Mom playgroup.

I can see it now. I stealthily creep into the tattoo parlor where all the butt-kicking Rocker Moms are busy banging their drum kits or polishing their Harleys. "Hey, guys," I would squeak. "Anyone up for Trivial Pursuit?" The peals of laughter would follow me out the door. It just wouldn't work.

Besides, my mom threw out the Sex Pistols jacket with great fanfare about twenty seconds after I left home for college.

So, where do I fit in? I think I can better relate to the distinctions between Geek Mom and Chic Mom. Guess which one I am. Here are some hints:

Even before I had a kid I preferred to stay home and watch *Shark Week* on a Saturday night, rather than go out for a twelve-dollar apple-tini.

I wear earth shoes, not stilettos. For all I know, Manolo Blahnik is a flavor of Ben and Jerry's ice cream.

My hair defies gravity. No matter how much I coat it with expensive, cruelty-free, organic pomade, wisps begin their voyage toward the ceiling before 10:00 a.m. By lunchtime the poof is fully unleashed and I resemble a radioactive poodle.

I am a fish-belly-white dough girl who spent her entire pubescent career, in the Texas sunshine, avoiding shorts. I have never been able to get a tan. I know, I know. It is better to save my precious skin from the evils of the sun. But, even when tans are not "in," they are still "in," if you know what I mean.

I am a *Star Wars* fanatic.

I overanalyze everything, from the pros and cons of cloth diapering to which set of tacky lingerie will best embarrass my sister at her bridal shower—hence, this exercise in self-indulgent babbling.

As you can see, the cards were stacked in favor of my becoming a Geek Mom. And now I have a precious little blank slate on which to transfer my utter geek-ness. My daughter already has a head start with her alabaster skin.

Let me now tell you about the moms who are the yin to my yang, the Chic Moms. The Chic Moms were all members of a special tribe, the Lint Free People, before they ever had kids.

Lint Free women always have smooth hair, glossed back into a shiny, bouncy ponytail. A Lint Free person never has tuna fish breath or a piece of used dental floss stuck to her rear end. She never shoots a dirty look at the unhelpful postal worker or forgets the name of her husband's co-worker. She never endures the endless round of daily mishaps that plague us geeks. In high school, she was Prom Queen. And very tan.

Of course, just like I retain my special geek status post-natal, so do the Lint Free People remain flawless once they cross the border into Mamaland. Even as moms, they artfully avoid wearing yogurt as a hairstyling product. Their nursing babies never pop off the breast at exactly the wrong moment, causing a geyser of milk to land on the nice gentleman across the restaurant.

I see the Chic Moms, the Lint Free ones, walking with their babies in the chi chi Marina neighborhood of San Francisco. The Chic Moms' bellies are toned and their Fendi diaperbags are immaculate. Their clothes match and they actually wear eye shadow. The chrome bars on their Peg Perrigo strollers shine as if their butlers have buffed them with Turtle Wax.

All right, all right. Before I get too catty, I'll stop and admit that deep down underneath their rouged exterior, the Chic Moms are probably full of screwed-up-ness and self-doubt, just like the rest of us.

Hormones, culture, and the whole biological urge to nurture do provide a bit of common ground for most of us good old American mamas. Although I often feel more like a freak than a geek in light of some of my more left-of-center parenting choices, I honestly like to (naively?) imagine that we mamas are more alike than we are different.

Isn't that a nice thought? The fantasy that we can put aside our categorizing and judging and join hands for a nice round of *It's a Small Mom World After All*. Considering the lack of institutionalized support that our society offers for the endless litany of mom-related issues, we sure could lean on each other a little bit more and pick at each other a little bit less. And it could start right here, with little ol' me.

Rocker Mom. Soccer Mom. Geek Mom. Chic Mom. I don't mean to blow your mind again, but notice a common theme?

That's right, Einstein! We've all emerged from a particularly rough diapering sesh with a hand smeared in poop. We've all gotten so fried from "negotiating" with a toddler that we've wanted to submerge our heads in a full bathtub while gurgling, "Calgon! Take me away!" And we've all experienced indescribable moments of nostalgia and joy when watching our babies sleep, overwhelmed by the rush of time that sends them hurtling from infancy into childhood.

Next time I feel the urge to box in my fellow mamas, it might do this geek some good to remember that.

One State, Two State, Red State, Blue State

Now that the 2004 election has passed, like many Americans, I want to look ahead and stop talking about our country like it is one of my daughter's Dr. Seuss books. I see no better way to work through my post-election angst than to plan a holiday visit to a town in West Texas called Midland.

Midland is the former home of President George W. and Laura Bush. It is also the former home of this here writer—and the current home of my parents, God bless their little red state souls.

Even though I am a card-carrying Democrat (of course I am—I live in San Francisco) and my folks are rabid Republicans (of course they are—they have lived in West Texas their whole lives, minus a stint in California in the 60's which failed to convert them into hippies), I look forward to hanging out in Midland with my family this Christmas. I hope that our celebration will help to bridge the cultural divide between we blues and reds.

It may be tough, as there exists a primordial snarl of political head butting between my Baby Boomer parents and their Gen X offspring.

Back in high school, my household had the distinction of receiving regular direct mail pieces from the National Rifle Association alongside gun-control fliers with headlines screaming that the NRA can stick their bullets where the sun don't shine. Pro-hunting organizations and People for the Ethical Treatment of Animals had us on their regular solicitation lists, no doubt causing our mail carrier to wonder what went on in the nuthouse at the end of the cul-de-sac.

More recently, on a trip back home shortly after the 2000 election, I discovered an invitation to W's inaugural ball, alongside a Bush family

Christmas card, proudly displayed on my folks' refrigerator. I made a big display of telling my mom that her attempt to show off her famous friend held no street cred with this (shall I dare say the dirty word?) Liberal, but she blew off her bleeding-heart daughter's soapbox rant.

So, as you can see, I don't go back to visit Midland because I fit right into the political climate, but rather because there are a few quirky things I love about what the locals call "The Tall City" of West Texas. Here are a couple of Midland holiday tidbits guaranteed to regularly astound my San Francisco friends:

Midland may very well be the only city in the world where tumbleweeds are both a dread enemy and an art form. Tumbleweeds, the dried up carcasses of some kind of thistle plant, have been know to pile up twenty-feet high against the doors of the Midland Mall after a particularly grueling windstorm. Terrified shoppers, who are trapped inside, must subsist on the remnants of food court deep fryer bins until the fire department arrives with axes.

On the upside, when Midland misses out on a white Christmas, due to Mother Nature's finicky relationship with cactus and oil derricks, children delight in stacking tumbleweeds into frayed, post-modern suggestions of real snowmen.

Midland is geographically flatter than an armadillo after Houston rush hour traffic, but it is full of people who love to snow ski. One Christmas, it actually snowed—precluding the need for Tumbleweed snowmen—and the snow stuck around, without melting, for longer than the typical two hours and forty minutes.

This was back in the 1980s, before the much-acclaimed Loop 250 Highway finally made its sorta-circle around Midland. As part of the stalled construction, big mounds of earth, intended as future overpasses, sat idle in between the lanes of the service road. Once the snow settled, people pulled out their skis and took a few runs on the powder-covered dirt piles that lined the streets. As the brave skiers risked life, limb and a possible citation (Midland cops aren't too busy), passing drivers leaned out of their pick-up trucks and gave whoops of encouragement.

Stories like these make me look forward to spending Christmas back in my hometown, where I never know who or what I might come across. In fact, the reality that one might randomly bump into the mighty handsome former Secretary of Commerce, Don Evans, might be why no self-respecting Midland woman dares to peek outside her door without full make-up and a carefully sprayed enormous hair-do.

I appreciate the fact that dear old Midland friends embrace my Left Coast family with open arms and a sincere "Welcome home, y'all!" If anyone cares that I rally around a political spectrum that is about as far away from Midland as Tokyo, they are at least polite enough to not make a big deal about it.

I can't wait to go there again this year, where I can forget about our nation's division as I sit by the fire with four generations of West Texas family. I hope that for a brief window of time, we will look beyond who voted for which rich white guy and just bask in the eggnog-soaked glow of what we value most—each other.

Hey, if my family can do it, maybe there is hope for our nation after all.

Gangsta Napper

We have a family secret. It involves the fact that every time I hear *In da Club* by 50 Cent, I think of the birth of my little girl, Grace. It was well timed by the fates that the gangsta rapper's meteoric single shot to the top of the charts along with Grace's entry into the world. Jeff "illegally" downloaded the song online, burned it to a CD and played it nonstop during the first few weeks of Grace's life outside the womb. It became a sort of inappropriate family lullaby, and we sang it to Grace at three in the morning when we all huddled in our double bed for bleary, hallucinogenic night feedings.

"Yo, Shorty, it's your birthday. We're gonna party like it's your birthday. Gonna sip Bacardi like it's your birthday," Jeff would gently bleat as he paced the floor and patted a confused and crying newborn, who, thank God, was too little to have acquired the language capacity to be corrupted by the rest of the lyrics.

In a classic white fratboy appropriation of ghetto rap, Jeff became obsessed with the song. It popped up every morning as we puttered around the kitchen, still recovering from our fitful sleepless night. He kept the download on his laptop where he pushed replay again and again as he worked his latest statistical analysis or caught up on emails from disgruntled students who were insensitive to paternity leave.

When we ventured out for family forays, for what seemed at the time to be essential baby supplies, up to the Citikids store on Clement Street or down to San Bruno to Lullaby Lane, 50 Cent blared from the speakers, the noise and car movement lulling Grace to sleep. I stared from the passenger window, watching the hills of San Francisco weave in and out of the fog, often unaware that I was chanting verses like, "I'm into having sex; I'm not into making love; So come give me a hug." Once I snapped out of my reverie, I would quickly scan the sidewalks to make sure no one I knew had seen me, overreacting to the fact that I was merely embarrassed by our choice of music.

I fluctuated between worry that rap music was too harsh for innocent baby ears and pride at the fact that my little one was already so multicultural. As a feminist, I don't openly admit to enjoying music that derides women as playthings for a singer's evening out in a bar, and I worried what my progressive mommy friends would think. In the end, exhaustion won the battle and I stopped caring what music she heard, as long as it comforted her during evening yell-a-thons.

Sometimes, in desperation I found myself mashing together verses from *Free to Be You and Me,* the Bee Gees, and Metallica as I frantically rocked, nursed, patted, swaddled, changed and calmed Miss Fussypants. No matter what cacophonic medley was created, by the end of the day an adult member of our household would always resort to the old stand-by, Mr. 50 Cent. When my mom came from Texas to give us a break, I tried to include her in our private baby soother and teach her the words. She was unappreciative of the fact that we let her in on our dirty little secret, and she chose to stick with the less hip *Rock-a-bye, baby.*

One day I was out in our old neighborhood, the Western Addition, when a car drove by with the kind of speakers that make San Franciscans think that the 1989 earthquake was just practice for this, the real thing. I saw that the car (or rather I felt the vibrations reset my heart rate a good ten minutes before I had a chance to view it) contained one middle-aged, very white looking fellow with slicked back hair and an earring. He had the windows rolled down, the base cranked up like he was auditioning to be Run-DMC's audio technician, and his head was jerking about like a Giants bobbler to the tune of (you guessed it) *In da Club.*

Even in my new parental out of touch with reality state, I knew that our family's hush-hush theme song was a top of the pops sensation. I was nonetheless shocked at the sight of the middle-aged goober who was attempting to jam to it. I stopped my stroller in mid push and gawked at the dude pretending to be a teenage boy in the hood. In this city I am quite used to seeing everything from bearded Asian drag queens dressed like Foxy Brown to shirtless runaways with pierced nipples and tattooed foreheads. It takes a lot to make me turn my head. But this guy was playing our baby's song, and I suddenly felt self-conscious about our regular ghetto-blasting of 50 Cent from the Honda. For about ten seconds I questioned the socialization of our baby into yet another wanna-be playa. However, this wore off by the time I got home and Grace needed Daddy to put her down for a nap. Whatever worked behind the closed doors of our flat was fine with me.

Having a baby is frightfully similar to getting married, in terms of commitment and also regarding the buckets of cash to be siphoned from the terror that both decisions provoke. When businesses and service-providers hear the magic word, "engagement," dollar signs suddenly light up in sales person's eyes and prices elevate by 2,000%.

Likewise, the baby industry is full of savage marketers who prey on the fears and insecurities of new parents. They try to convince us that we need things like mechanical lifelike teddy bears that emanate calming music and vibrate in mimicry of the womb, or special baby aromatherapy calf massage cream. My early days with Baby Grace taught me that we didn't need any of that crap. Our happiest times were simple: we needed diapers, Mommy's boobies, some loving arms, and a healthy dose of our hush-hush family spokesperson, 50 Cent.

Hey Neighbor! Can I Borrow A Cup of Crack?

My baby's first neighbors were drug addicts. I guess they were not exactly neighbors in the official, legal sense, but I feel confident about the drug part. Technically they fell into the category of "squatters", but they did most of their living within twenty yards of our kitchen.

In the 1950s, our Victorian house on San Francisco's historic Alamo Square had been chopped into four individual flats with a couple of non-residential storage rooms underneath. Our photo-friendly location marked a primo tour bus stop, with the famous "Painted Ladies" as our neighbors. We also had quick access to Haight-Ashbury, birthplace of the Grateful Dead, and the Castro, the gayest hood in America, with limitless opportunities for drinking, dining, dancing and shopping. Dino, our beatnik Daddy-O landlord, carefully selected all of the tenants on what he believed to be a hepcat blend of character traits and groovy personalities. We loved our charming flat and we thought we had struck habitat gold.

And for a while we did live in the mother lode. Our building housed Dino's dream mix of creative, urban professionals, and we all got along beautifully. Casual chitchat peppered the front stoop, invitations to parties were frequent, and we often left homemade cookies on each other's doorsteps. When Grace, our baby, was born, the other tenants elected her building mascot, and showered her with coos and affection. Randy, Dino's on-again, off-again handyman, lurked about now and then, but, naive in our neighborly bliss, we initially neglected to see the warning signs of his sneaky residency.

Randy reminded me of a gray-haired, strung-out version of Schneider from Valerie Bertinelli's TV hit, *One Day at A Time,* complete with a dirty white t-shirt and tool belt. His white mustache usually retained crumbs from yesterday's breakfast, and his stiff hair too closely resembled Donald Trump's mysterious coif, sans the Wall Street panache. Most like Schneider, he was always hanging around, although he didn't come in through the window. He rented one of the basement storage rooms that had its entrance through our backyard, and he used the room for some sort of enigmatic workshop. Boxes of Randy's stuff littered the back garden, and I often heard him using unidentifiable electric power tools for hours on end. He gave me the royal heebie jeebies, even before I surmised that he spent most of his nights illegally shacked up on the basement floor, but his status as our fixer-upper earned him some space and rights to make a mess.

Randy's white, serial-killer panel van, with all its windows painted shut, often blocked the garage where our neighbors kept their cars. The driveway block is a major violation of San Francisco parking etiquette, and on many mornings they blasted their horns to rouse Randy to come move his mystery machine. The fact that he came shuffling from his backyard basement hideaway at 7:30 a.m. was our first clue that something was afoot with this handyman gone awry, but we naively simply assumed he was an industrious guy who took his handyman job seriously. Gradually, the warning signs piled up and the tenants started keeping their heads up for more shenanigans.

They weren't too hard to find. The platonic gay roomies, who lived right above Randy's lair, swore that they heard a television blaring well into the night. Phil, the hyperactive building manager, peeked into Randy's basement one day when Randy wasn't around. Randy's trappings: a mattress on the floor, the confirmed TV, drug paraphernalia, and boxes and boxes of crap, gave Phil the willies, and he pounced on Dino to get an eviction, and *pronto.*

Evictions take a long time to process in tenant-friendly San Francisco. While we waited to hear if Randy would get the boot, we had the joy of becoming well acquainted with the chemically imbalanced radiance of Randy's lovely Better Half, who seemed to have nowhere better to go than our house. One of the bartender guys from upstairs conferred upon her the moniker of "Crackety Crackhead." My husband, Jeff, and I, having been raised in genteel Texas, and taught to abide by certain standards of formality in manners, simply anointed her "Mrs. Randy." We especially didn't want to offend any crack users who weren't actual "Crackheads."

Mrs. Randy wandered the sidewalks in front of our building, drinking giant three liter bottles of generic brand orange soda and yelling to the sky.

And if Randy's crunch-tastic hairdo needed a good conditioning, then Mrs. Randy gave a whole new meaning to the phrase "styled with an eggbeater."

Her sweatpants were usually pulled up to her thighs, exposing her dirt-encrusted, unshod feet, furry calves and scabby knees. Keep in mind that we lived along a well-traveled urban footpath where it was not unusual to step in any number of bodily excretions, both animal and human. Mrs. Randy's feet slapped happily along the filthy thoroughfare as if we lived in suburban Orange County and the sidewalks were tidy manicured lawns. We had no confirmation of where she came from or where she slept, but all signs pointed to Randy's spooky lair.

The graphic designer who worked from home in one of the upstairs units, confirmed this suspicion when he started seeing Mrs. Randy wandering around the back garden at all hours of day and night, one time with curlers in her hair. Although not all of my questions were answered, I finally had an insight into how she maintained that fresh from the salon look.

Once, I tried to sneak past Mrs. Randy when taking Grace out for a walk, but I had no such luck. As soon as I tiptoed over the threshold, Mrs. Randy jumped up from the anthill she sat on, and yelled, "How is your day today???!" with eyes wilder than a caged hyena. I stared at the ground and muttered a soft, "Fine, thanks," before scurrying away, all the while saying a silent prayer that her deranged vibes wouldn't rub off on my clean-souled little baby.

It all came to a head one day when I was home alone with Grace. Overcome with a bout of mania, Mrs. Randy spent the afternoon standing guard in front of our house, metal rake in hand. She scraped the already spotless sidewalk for hours, creating a bone-chilling repetition akin to the proverbial nails on the chalkboard. Once she had sufficiently removed the imaginary debris from the cement, she raked most of the bark off the lower half of the lone tree that sprouted from the concrete in front of our stoop. Then she turned her delirium to the house itself and proceeded to scrape the side of the building for what seemed like several years.

Trapped in my flat, I huddled with Grace as the horror-show *scrape, scrape, scrape* gradually eroded my sanity. An obviously off-balance woman carrying a pronged, metal weapon lurked just outside my door, and I was too terrified to leave the house. Even the cats went nuts. Thinking that the scratchy noises came from rat toenails inside the walls, they howled in anticipation of a hunt, adding to my tension.

By some miracle of chance, Dino happened to stop by the building, and I heard him yell at Mrs. Randy to make like Michael Jackson and beat it. In response to Dino's admonishment, Mrs. Randy whined, in a surprisingly nasal Brooklyn accent, "Awww, geee, Dino! WhadidIdooooowrooong?"

I suppressed an urge to lean out the window and enumerate her many wrongdoings, starting with those wormy feet.

Mrs. Randy and her rake soon disappeared, but the saga was not over yet. Thinking that it was safe to finally get some non-crazy fresh air, Grace and I emerged from the apartment. We sat on the front stoop to wait for Jeff to get home from work, and I anticipated telling him a story that described more than the volume and consistency of various baby excretions. Suddenly a cop pulled into the driveway and got out of the car.

"Are you the one who called the police?" he asked.

I shook my head dumbly, but before I could open my mouth, Phil, the hyperactive building manager who initiated Randy's eviction, roared up to the house in his Jeep Grand Cherokee. He practically frothed at the mouth as he leapt from the SUV and ran up to the porch. "I saw it again today! They're living down there! I know they are!" He panted, "It's drugs! Definitely drugs!!"

I held Grace tight as I watched Frothy Phil and the policeman go around to the backyard. I expected them to come out dragging Mr. or Mrs. Randy, but they didn't. Instead they returned with a freshly cuffed new person. Not Randy. Not Mrs. Randy. But a brand new guest.

The strange woman wore a filthy blue parka and flannel pajama bottoms. Her hair looked like it could have benefited from a round with Mrs. Randy's curlers. She kept mumbling, "I'm just waiting for Randy. He said I could look at TV." I stared in amazement, processing the fact that not two, but at least three drug addicts lived under my floorboards. I cautiously peered around the side of the house, wondering who else lived back there. At that point, I would not have been shocked if Rush Limbaugh came wandering through the gate, tweaking for his next fix.

Jeff had the precision timing to arrive home from work right as all of the police action went down. Imagine a loving daddy, excited to escape the daily grind, being greeted not by a sexy wife and adorable offspring, but by the following melee: Phil, sweating, screeching, and flailing his arms like he had just single-handedly won the war on drugs; a police cruiser parked in the driveway, its driver calmly escorting a tricked-out looking woman who had apparently just stopped by our basement for some Must See TV; me, wearing unwashed yoga pants, my hair piled on top of my head like I took styling lessons from Mrs. Randy, with one breast hanging a nipple too close to the edge of my unlatched nursing bra; and Grace, absorbing this highly-charged scene with her until-then untainted, six-month-old eyes.

Jeff and I spent the evening debating the pros and cons of moving out of the Randy house. With hindsight, weighing the pain-in-the-butt of finding a new place, the expense and time of executing the actual move, against our child's potential for finding a crackpipe in the garden seemed like a no-brainer. However, the small town yokels that still lurked within us found vindication of our coolness in our awesome tourist-central Frisco dwelling. A claw-foot tub, antique wainscoting, and the San Francisco equivalent of living near the Eiffel Tower were bragging points when we hosted our Texas pre-fab, subdivision-dwelling friends.

I also fought an inner battle against the conservative West Texas shell from which I sprung. I have shunned the Republicanism of my upbringing with great pride, and my urge to run away shamed the liberal in me. I told myself that I should be more compassionate toward the poor and disenfranchised. More loving and kind to the Randy clan. I asked myself, "What would Bill Clinton do?"

Being a mama intensified this identity struggle. The animal need to protect my offspring found refuge in the sheltered Texas girl of my youth and threatened to shut down the wanna-be urban cool kid that I had nurtured for so long. Our Randy situation threw all of these aspects of my personality into the blender, churning up insecurities and future therapy bills

That same night someone rang our doorbell at three in the morning looking for Randy, and the camel's back came crunching down under the weight of that very heavy piece of straw. Being a protective mama suddenly took first place in my identity queue, bypassing "socially progressive" and "open-minded" by a wide margin.

It was time to move the hell out of a crackhouse and find a place suitable for raising a child.

Although we threw off the charmed balance of our lovely tenant community—the last time we drove by I saw our old windows lined with aluminum foil—we decided to schlep ourselves and our possessions to a new flat that had less proximity to Randy-style hijinks.

I know that not all families can escape such sketchy situations. I am grateful that we had the resources to move to a more kiddo-friendly section of the city, where the only chemical abuse in our house comes from Daddy spraying too much WD-40 on the creaky hinges. In time, we'll tell Grace of this seedier life we briefly lived, and in time she'll experience similar absurdities, but for now we're happy to do it without having junkies living in the basement.

Until then, Sayanora, Crackheads!

You Say You Want a Resolution?

Maybe I had too much time on my hands during our holiday travels. While vacationing in my Texas hometown, I took a solitary trip to the grocery store, where I spent several blissful, childfree minutes buying diapers, packets of baby yogurt, and a new sippy cup. My daughter, Grace, enjoyed the break too, as she stayed behind to romp around the Christmas tree with her grandparents while I reveled in the free babysitting.

I was not sure how the heck to handle myself in a checkout line without the company of a screeching toddler chewing through a shopping cart handle or hurling half-chewed crackers into the hair of the cashier. So I restlessly hopped from foot to foot while scrutinizing the headlines from women's magazines that I rarely have time to read anymore.

Inspired by the litany of "New Year/New You!" self-improvement possibilities—aspirations as predictable as momentous sex life improvements and unrealistic thigh circumference reductions—promised on the glossy covers, I decided to forge ahead with my own itinerary for 2005. I rushed back to my folks' house and hurriedly scribbled a list of New Year's resolutions on the back of a scrap of wrapping paper. I came up with a challenging set of goals that still seemed deliciously within my meager reach.

Here it is:

Diet: Eat something green more than once a week. We're talking veggies here. St. Patrick's Day-dyed beer, green M & M's, and moldy Brie do not count.

Hygiene: Shower daily. With soap, if possible.

Beauty: Cover the Bride-of-Frankenstein dark circles under my eyes with concealer at least three days per week.

Home Improvement: Rinse off the scraps of apple that Grace throws on the floor before surreptitiously scooping them up and stuffing them in my mouth, which is always closer than the trashcan.

Therapy: Cuddle and pet our two cats, who have been relegated to second-class citizens in our house since the advent of the kiddo, for thirty minutes each and every day.

Health: Make long-overdue dental appointment to have my crusty molars scraped clean.

Fitness: When jogging with my mama friends, quit faking that Grace threw a toy from the jog stroller each time we embark on a particularly steep San Francisco hill.

When I showed my list to my mom she offered me some time worn advice.

"Honey, I think you sell yourself a little short," she cooed in her honey-coated southern drawl. "You can do much more than that if you put your mind to it."

These are the same sage words she shared with me when I traipsed home from my new wave stylist's Depeche Mode-blaring hair salon, circa 1988. Having outgrown my provincial high school scene at the ripe old age of fifteen, I boldly pronounced to my mother that I planned to make a career of being a professional shampoo girl.

Mom was right about my hair-washing ambition. I did spend a few years as a professional woman who actually wore suits and heels, out-earning my grad-student spouse. So I took Mom's advice the second time around and spruced up my goals. I kept the pushy women's mags in mind and gave myself a metaphorical kick in the booty.

Here is what I added:

Health: Stop staying up until 2:00 a.m. watching *Will and Grace*, especially when I know that Grace will be up at 5:30 the next morning.

Home Improvement: Clean the ancient spider webs out of the bowels of our garage before they become designated as San Francisco historical landmarks.

Parenting: Organize Grace's toys by color, type, and frequency of use.

Parenting, Part II: Rotate said toys to achieve maximum toddler brain stimulation.

Fitness: Run, lift weights, practice yoga, and get generally as cut and buff as Tea Leone in time for swimsuit season.

Social Activism: Elevate the status of stay-at-home-parent to a level that gets at least as much respect as a fake blond heiress who stars in her own homemade porn.

Community Service: Volunteer to assist our hunky mayor, Gavin Newsom, in solving San Francisco's homeless problem.

Career: Write great American novel.

Contribution to Humanity: Achieve world peace.

I think I got a little carried away. Especially since the last few on the list are about as possible as evicting the spiders whose ancestors settled in our home during the 1849 Gold Rush. Even though Mom gave me some dead-on advice, I didn't want to set myself up to fail by creating a list that reflected lack of sleep hallucinations more than realistic expectations.

Screw the magazines, I thought, and I gave my resolutions one more try. I think that the final revision truly distills the essence of life in my house these days. And to be honest, if I achieve just a couple of the goals of my 2005 Self-Improvement Program, I will probably run into the street, throw a beret into the air and scream, "She just might make it after all!" like Mary Tyler Moore in my favorite Nick at Nite show.

Here is the final draft:

Hygiene: Shower 6 out of 7 days a week.

Home Improvement: Don't wait for the catbox to grow legs and meow at the door before scooping it.

Beauty: Try to find the concealer for those undereye circles. (Grace probably threw it under the sofa or behind the toilet.)

Health: Floss sometimes, and think really good thoughts about my teeth.

Therapy: Stop reading women's magazines that make me feel like an inferior slob who can't afford this season's must-have microscopic clutch purse that's a "Steal!" at $250.

Contribution to Self and Family: Go to bed each night knowing that I am blessed and lucky.

Lessons From a Little Nut

"How 'bout....go shopping?"

My daughter's blue eyes popped wide open with sincerity as she made this unexpected request. In shock, I momentarily forgot my half-hour long struggle to get her to take a dang nap. I stared in amazement.

My God, she wants to go shopping! I thought. Where the heck did little Grace learn to say such a thing?

No doubt she was only repeating something heard around the house in the midst of holiday hoopla. I was nonetheless astounded that my child could so cleverly try to finagle getting out of a nap by suggesting that we take a jaunt to the Gap.

My astonishment arose from the fact that, once again, parenthood brought a cliché to life. I used to watch a TV show, hosted by Bill Cosby. I think it was called *Kids Say the Darnedest Things*. It consisted of the Coz grilling a menagerie of dimpled charmers who quipped off double-entendres and misinformation about anatomy. It was full of gems like, "My mommy is going to the hospital to have the baby come out of her Virginia."

This brainless show appealed to a primordial sense of humor that I share with my otherwise cerebral hubby, Jeff. It is hardcore, no-thought-required, downright stoopid humor, just like another winner, *America's Funniest Home Videos*. A key difference in the two shows is, of course, *AFV's* tendency to showcase a gut-busting, knee-slapping montage of men smashing their gonads on run-amuck vacuum cleaners and the business ends of powerboats.

But I digress. Although I once loved Cosby's clever banter with the pre-K set, I took the show to be staged, a fakeroo. Now that I am the mama of a newly jabbering tyke, I understand that you can't make this stuff up.

I should have gotten a clue a few years back. Jeff and I spent the weekend at a ranch house in the Texas hill country with good friends and their three-year old son. One night as we all sat out by the campfire, roasting marshmallows, our flashlight suddenly went kaput.

Our hosts went off in search of a new flashlight, leaving their son, Nate, out by the campfire with Jeff and me. Jeff, thinking this a prime time to teach young Nate about the ways of the world, launched into a long-winded metaphor that ultimately compared the busted flashlight to a car that needed gasoline.

As Jeff finished his diatribe, three-year-old Nate soulfully looked up from his perch by the dwindling flames. He took in Jeff's astute nugget of information, the wonder in his wide eyes reflecting the glow of the orange embers.

"No," he said, "It just needs batteries." He might as well have added, "You dumbass."

Perhaps, as non-parents, we too quickly chose to forget Nate's shaming of Jeff, because Grace's simple pronouncements continue to stop us in our tracks. Her tiny, thoughtful statements often resemble proverbs culled from wizened philosophers of eras gone by.

I have heard toddler speak described as the "Little Buddha" stage, because of this ability to convey so much with so few words. I couldn't agree more. Consider these other lessons to be learned from my daughter's sage bits of prose:

While visiting family over the holidays, we took a walk along the banks of Lake Nasworthy, outside of San Angelo, Texas. Jeff and I hoofed along like yuppies on treadmills, but Grace meandered to and fro, checking out the subtle nuances of groundcover along the way. At one point she stopped, squatted down, and patted the earth beneath her feet.

"I like this dirt!" she proclaimed, then looked up to make sure that Mama and Daddy saw her object of appreciation.

I stared at the damp, red circle on which she squatted and remembered when it felt good to rub my hands in something nice and gritty, when the sensation of dirt under my nails did not evoke the immediate need for a manicure.

We don't have a lot of dirt where we play in San Francisco. Our microscopic back garden hosts flagstones, weeds, and an infestation of never-ending spider webs. Wide sidewalks and asphalt surround our house. Our playground refuge has lots of sand, but no honest-to-goodness dirt. For that we must venture into the questionable area of the park's dog run, where poop, broken glass and who knows what else awaits her tiny hands.

Yes, I thought. I like this dirt too. Thanks for the reminder, kid.

Another lesson came in the form of a Christmas stocking stuffer request. Over the years, my mom has created beautiful hand-stitched stockings, personalized for each member of our family. This Christmas, Grace stared at them, enraptured by the swirls of brightly colored thread. We explained, several times, how we load up the stockings with special gifts, and I think Grace caught on.

When I finally asked her, "Grace, what would you like in your stocking?" she replied, "Little nut."

The simplicity of her request was refreshing and comforting in the face of the mass consumerism that Jeff and I constantly fight to keep away from our toddler. I know that she will soon begin her demands for Archeologist Barbie or SpongeBob Squarepants Beginning Dentistry Kit, but thank God she is still immune to the ooze of child-directing marketing.

Little nut. Simple. Basic. Easy to accommodate and reflective of one of Grace's favorite snacks. On Christmas morning, Grace reached into her stocking, her mouth opened wide in amazement, and she gasped with joy as she pulled out a baggie full of little nuts.

It reminded me to be grateful for those core blessings during the holidays. Good company, good food, and, if I am lucky, a special treat, like a little nut.

So, what about the "go shopping" request? Since Grace now repeats after me, I have to not only watch my potty mouth language, but also keep my greed in check. If I want to raise a girl whose self-esteem runs deeper than how good she looks in her jeans, I'd better model that in both words and behavior. Wouldn't it be nice if the next time Grace tries to sneak out of taking a nap she says, "How 'bout go volunteer?"

But, then again, life is a balance between caring for others and sometimes pampering ourselves. As Grace gets a little older I may cash in on her recent suggestion and celebrate a special event with some good old mother-daughter bonding through consumerism.

It won't be too hard to utter the words, "How 'bout go shopping?"

Invitation to the Donner Party

A sign marked the site where the infamous Donner Party spent a horrific winter stranded in the Sierra Nevadas. But it was buried in snow.

Perhaps a bad omen? I tried not to think about it and instead kept my gaze on the glorious, snow-covered trees lining the highway.

"Oooohhh!!" I squealed to my daughter forcing my own distraction from the dangerous driving conditions. "Look at the pretty snow! It is white and cold!" Painfully obvious, I know. But I desperately needed to focus on something other than being lost and starving in a blizzard.

Oblivious to the winter wonderland that furiously encircled our rented behemoth Yukon, Grace again pushed the button on her sing-along *Blue's Clues* storybook. She swayed her head gently from side to side, enjoying the electronic rhythms of *Twinkle Twinkle Little Star*. So sweet and content, unaware of the ice and sleet that threatened our solid vehicle.

I was glad she couldn't feel my tension regarding the symbolism of the historical landmark we crawled past. Remember the Donner Party? The most famous band of pioneers to ever head west? They got stuck in a snowstorm and had to eat each other. I couldn't stop thinking about their awful fate, having no solid, gas-guzzling SUV to protect them from their inevitable, gruesome end. My stomach felt a little queasy at the thought of their human menu.

"Ok!" I yelled into the SUV full of my in-laws. "If we get stuck, no one can eat Grace!" My feeble attempt to break the tension was met with a hearty guffaw from Jeff's step-mom. His dad, our fearless driver, continued to stare at the icy road. Jeff's little brother sat in the very back of the car, along with the Panamanian foreign exchange student who lives with my in-laws. The young boys were each plugged into their iPods, perhaps less tense than me, and they missed my tacky cannibal joke.

Our merry band of travelers headed out of California, on our way to Tahoe, for a week of bone-cracking skiing and snowboarding. We only had one booger up the nose of our otherwise lovely vacation. We had to pass through the biggest blizzard to hit the California-Nevada border since the Donners fired up the human barbeque.

My friends at home in San Francisco were astounded at our bravery. That we had the guts to get out in the nastiest weather this side of the arctic tundra. It had rained buckets for days in the City, turning my world into steep slippery streets, washed-out playgrounds, and frantic housebound children.

Desperate to get our Play-doh-eating tots out of the house, my friends pulled together a field trip to a local museum. But we were too busy packing to join the fun.

"Sorry, Sheila. I can't go to the museum today. I am going to put my child in the car and drive on the Interstate in the worst storm to hit Northern California since 1919."

Ok, so I didn't actually say that. But I might as well have.

We made it by the Donner Pass without having to eat anyone. But it was a close call.

The night before, road closures halted our journey, and we shacked up at a hotel in Auburn, California. Shortly after we ordered takeout, the storm caused the electricity to fizzle and die. Much to Grace's delight, we ate our droopy pizza in the hallway. Jeff scrounged up some beer from what he called the saddest grocery store he had ever seen.

"I think it is where groceries go to die," he solemnly declared, before opening an ancient bottle.

The spastic blinking of the flashlight, Grace's newfound favorite toy, blended eerily with the yellow glowing emergency light system. We lounged in the generated haze and joked about the teenage girls who ran giggling up and down the hall in hopes of catching the attention of my collegiate brother-in-law. We laughed at how Jeff and his dad almost got caught in the elevator when the power went out.

But underneath the jovial banter, I thought about families who made snowy journeys in the past, who did not have the comforts of Holiday Inn and skunky beer when the weather turned rough.

Unlike some of the Donners, we finally made it to our destination in one piece.

The first morning in Tahoe, all the adults headed to the slopes except me. As usual, I was key person on child duty. No matter. I couldn't wait to share my love of winter sports with my daughter. As gung ho as a ski bunny on steroids, I loaded up Grace on the resort shuttle and headed out for a day of sledding.

And I learned something very important that day. Grace hates snow.

Her avalanche-inducing screeches bounced off the walls of the canyon before I could force her onto the bright orange toboggan: "Grace HOLD Mommy! Grace HOLD Mommy!" (Translation: "Mom, will you please carry me?")

Amused skiers traipsed by on their way to the lift. Oblivious young snowboarders sprayed powder in my face as I perched on the plastic sled and screamed, "Watch Mommy. Look how fun!!! WATCH MOMMY DO IT!!!"

No matter how many times I rolled in the snow, she refused to try.

Defeated, I went back to the condo, which was warm and cozy, isolated from the wind and snow that terrified my daughter.

Once safely inside, we stood together and stared out the sliding glass door. The Sierra Nevadas loomed, as powerful as gods, for miles and miles, certain of their might and permanence in the face of us puny mortals. I leaned down to kiss Grace's pink cheeks in wonder and gratitude. Just like me, she must often feel small in the face of this Earth, and I need to respect her wish to go slowly when faced with its awe.

Besides, the intensity of the snow spooked me too. Only my fear occurred back in the car, not when trying to ride my tush down the side of a mountain.

When we returned to San Francisco, the rains had stopped. The view from the Bay Bridge into the City was like the art on a cheesy religious greeting card. Brilliant orange shafts of sunshine streaked through the breaking clouds, offering a peek at a silken sky.

The next morning, Grace and I headed out to the nearest park. No snow there to make her scream or Mama worry.

We quickly ran into some neighborhood friends and made plans for a dinner party. I thought back on my recent case of the snow-traveling heebie jeebies, on the spooky reminder of the Donner Party and their horrible fate. The feeling of nausea, again, swelled in my throat. Thank God our friends are vegetarian.

Melons in the Mission

The coolest place I breastfed my daughter, Grace, was the bathroom in a Tapas bar in the Mission neighborhood of San Francisco.

San Francisco culture is a little bit neighborhood-centric. Folks readily self-identify with a particular pocket of the City, and stereotypes of the various sub-villages abound. There is the predictable, with posh yuppies in the Marina, and the fabulous, with the wildly gay Castro. Other neighborhood cultures include baby and dog-friendly Noe Valley, the South of Market warehouses and leather fetish bars, and the old-moneyed mansions of Pacific Heights.

The Mission neighborhood is a bustling community of Latin Americans and recent immigrants. When wandering this part of town, expect to hear people speaking Spanish and smell the spicy offerings from the many taquerias. Colorful shops sell everything from Panamanian soccer jerseys to customized piñatas.

The Mission also boasts some seriously hip hipsters—people so hip they put the most indie-punk garage bands to shame. I'm talking legwarmers and enormous sunglasses before they became retro-cool, tattoos (with phrases like "I Rule") before they darkened the ankles of frat boys. Fashion trends hit the Mission five years before they reach Midwestern universities.

Ironic t-shirts, vintage blazers, and authentic Converse sneakers are the uniform de rigueur for these cats who live on the cutting edge of all things next year. So a throng of rockin' bars and restaurants also crowd the Mission, catering to the shaggy-haired scenesters.

My sister, Lara, and her then-boyfriend, Steven, who closely resembled the above-mentioned hipsters, came to visit when Grace was a few months old. In attempt to hide my eternal geekiness and fake like I knew how to be cool in the City, I took them thrift-store shopping in the Mission.

This was not an easy task when I had a new baby who loved nothing more than slurping mama's homemade nectar in the tranquility of a quiet bedroom. For much of the afternoon, Jeff diligently held a screaming Grace while I hid in dressing rooms and pretended that my life did not revolve around diapers and breastpads. Amidst the roar of bands like Death Cab for Cutie and Interpol, I forced my swollen breasts into too-tight vintage cowboy shirts and popped more than one button on Dickies workpants designed for non-maternal bodies.

Tired of waiting around, Lara and Steven did what any self-respecting non-parents would do. They popped into a nearby yummy Tapas bar for a drink. I can't blame them for not considering the needs of a baby and choosing bar stools instead of a booth.

My small tribe, still in recovery from our dressing room fracas, soon made our way into the bar and joined the leisurely, childless couple.

Being an insecure new mom and not wanting to draw more attention to my yelling baby, I decided against rocking the boat by insisting on a more comfortable location. Instead, I balanced on the backless vinyl seat and pulled out an engorged breast to feed my worked-up girl. Still self-conscious about public nursing, I hoped that the suave, sideburned bartender would keep his focus on the pitcher of sangria he stirred, and not my attempt at discreet babyfeeding.

At this time in my Mama career, I suffered painful, over-productive breasts. I use the word "engorged" to describe my breasts because they were, well, engorged. My post-partum nurse at the hospital said they would simmer down in a couple of days. Nearly eight weeks later I still swelled to capacity with nature's best baby food and cursed that damn nurse for leading me on.

Imagine the most hard, firm, solid, round cantaloupes you have ever seen, sitting on a woman's chest like water balloons about to burst. Those were my breasts. Consequent to this cantaloupe-ism, there arose a little problem each time Grace nursed. The milk kind of squirted.

Ok, perhaps I do not do this squirting justice. Perhaps I should say that the milk full-on sprayed like a fire hydrant busted open by a gang of 1950s street urchins. Like a Dr. Pepper bottle shaken to its bursting point. Like Old Faithful.

Each time my sweet newborn clamped down her hungry lips, the flood of milk inevitably bum-rushed her mouth. Coughing and sputtering, she had to dismount and wait for the deluge to dwindle. Immediate mess issues aside, I worried about implications for Grace's college life. She already had an excellent tutorial that could serve well in future beer-bonging.

That day in the Mission bar, perched on the slippery barstool, was no different. As soon as my cranky girl got her latch on, I squirted like an overheated water pick. If Grace's mouth hadn't blocked the flow, I might have accidentally sauced up the pitcher of sangria with more than the requisite fruit slices.

Back then I still had the New Mama Hang Ups. Nowadays, if I had to feed a baby in such a situation, I would chuckle at its silliness and demand that we move to a private booth. That day, however, such action was unthinkable.

Thus, I freaked. In a mad rush of wetness and embarrassment, I grabbed the baby and dashed to the restroom.

I use "restroom" lightly here. It was a room. And the most drunken guest may have at one time chosen to rest in it. However, I surmise that most users of this four-foot squared hovel probably spent their time squatting above the suspicious commode, trying mightily not to touch anything.

This toilet—the only perch other than the questionable floor—had no lid, just the seat. Having yet to master any La Leche League-inspired, stand-up nursing, I plopped my clothed bottom down on the loo and smushed Grace into the spray. In a bout of sisterly sympathy, Lara ran in after me. She hovered about, offering paper towels and wisecracks.

We finally emerged from the bathroom: Me, with a milk soaked blouse and telltale ring on the rear of my khakis; Lara, with an expression suggesting plans for four kinds of birth control or else abstinence for life; and Grace, swooning with post-nursing bliss.

When I said that this place was the coolest nursing location in my baby's early days, I didn't mean cleanest or most comfortable. I mean that my baby saw a rockin' side of San Francisco, still new and exciting to Mama since I was pregnant when we moved here. Grace got to nurse in a bathroom where some pretentious scenester may have touched up her MAC lip-gloss or puked her bulimic guts out.

A few months later I returned to the hipster restaurant on a mama's night out, and I re-visited the same scary bathroom. The memories resurfaced like the gush from an over-productive breast.

What the hell was I thinking, nursing a baby in this nasty place, I thought.

Someday I may share this tale of breastfeeding hipness with Grace. But by then it may not sound so darn cool. Instead it might be like my parents' generation thinking it rocked to take a baby to a Peter, Paul and Mary concert.

By the time Grace is old enough to know about the coolness of the Mission, it may be so passé that I might as well be playing up the cultural relevance of Milli Vanilli. Of course, by then, Milli Vanilli will probably be retro-cool.

It's a Sling Thing

When I became a parent, my traditional accoutrements of seductive or tailored femininity went by the wayside. Necklaces became pull toys for busy, exploring hands. Scarves served as nooses for strangling mama. Gabardine blazers, cashmere ponchos, silk wraps—all were covered in puke, breastmilk, urine, or some combination of the above. I stuffed these accessories into the back of my closet, along with any expectations of sartorial beauty.

At least, that's how it went down in my house. I have witnessed new mamas who still wear dangly earrings and matching socks, but that was not my experience. Most of the time, when I hovered about my daughter, Grace, I considered my day a success if I remembered to wear deodorant. And the only pre-pregnancy clothes that fit me were the ones with grandma-style elastic waistbands. Then, a girlfriend who had started her own business making fabulous baby slings gave me one of her topnotch beauties as a welcome-baby gift. This time-tested baby carrier rapidly became my most prized fashion embellishment.

To the non-parent, it may sound a bit odd to say that my most precious fashion item held a baby. (At least I'm not completely cheesing out by suggesting that my best accessory was the baby herself.) But unlike many baby carriers, their fabrics printed with tacky ducky and teddy-bear designs, this sling rocked. It featured Chinese silk brocade in a vivid sage green—intense but not gaudy. Tiny white and yellow flowers and vines embellished the luxurious cloth, creating a look that was eye-catching yet classic. Never mind that this elegant sack held my cherished offspring—the container itself transformed me from frumpy, sleep-deprived matron into hip and sassy mama.

The exquisite baby carrier replaced my need for real accessories. Most of the time, I threw it on over jeans and a dirty white T-shirt for a quick walk around my San Francisco neighborhood. The silky fabric hid my grubby-housewife ensemble and distracted any onlookers from the ever-present circles of leaking breastmilk that stained my shirts.

I delighted in the attention given not just to my baby but to her carrier. Of course, fellow-mothers often stopped me to ask where I'd found such a lovely thing, but I also got a fair share of compliments from unexpected admirers. The blue-haired barista at the corner coffeehouse regularly cooed at my hipster sling, and the guy who lived above us begged to know where I'd found the fabric. (He needed to score a few yards to make a shirt for his boyfriend.)

My sling bolstered my delicate ego, still floundering in the face of my momentous life transition. It added a bit of flair and panache to stinky yoga pants or rumpled pajamas. It even saved the day on the occasion of a fashion crisis.

When Grace was about eight weeks old, we had plans to attend a wedding. In honor of the affair, and desperate to celebrate my bidding good riddance to maternity clothes, I bought a new skirt and blouse. On the day of the event, already decked out in my new party duds, I sat down in the rocking chair to give Grace a quickie feeding before we left the house. That nursing session triggered a gastrointestinal event of Biblical proportions as Grace experienced one of those nuclear-explosion–style poops. It leaked out of her diaper and all over my new outfit.

Panicked and late, I threw on a stretchy knit skirt and a shapeless, sleeveless sweater, then rushed out the door to the wedding. I sat in the back row of the Haight-Ashbury Catholic Church, smoldering with my own self-labeling: Ugly. Frazzled. Envious of the nonmaternal women who filled out their strapless dresses with curvaceous ease.

Later, at the reception, we got out of the car and I placed my sling over my sad ensemble. Grace snuggled inside, ready to snooze while her mama worked the room, and we entered the reception hall.

Something magical happened. Maybe it was my imagination, but I like to think my fancy green sling transformed me a bit that day. Its shine illuminated my curly red hair, still thick from pregnancy hormones. The fabric disguised the postpartum spare tire that encircled my waist. My cheeks, flushed with the music and chatter, reflected my illustrious silken ornament, and my eyes sparkled with laughter. The whole room stared at me, admiring the beautiful new mother with the gorgeous baby sling.

Although I still sorely missed my expensive wraps and delicate jewelry, for that small window of time I didn't care. I knew that I'd get them all back someday, and that my sling's hour of glory was fleeting. Like the finite nature of babyhood, it was meant to be part of my life for only a precious window of time before it took its turn at the back of my closet.

And, when Grace got a little older, it felt great to finally pull out some of my pre-baby accessories. But somehow, none of them has ever felt as beautiful as my sling.

Diaper Karma

I have no desire to wash cloth diapers, yet I love having cushy, natural padding against my little one's bum. So every Tuesday morning I put a bag of dirty cloth diapers on our front porch. The diaper service truck then swings by to pick up the yuckies, leaving behind fresh, clean diapers.

This simple transaction usually goes off without a hitch. But there was this one time...

Our old San Francisco neighborhood was a bit rough around the edges, a place where I first learned the word "gentrification." Graffiti and tired liquor stores juxtaposed renovated Victorians and weekend yuppies. Before we moved away from this old 'hood, my family had a curious cloth diaper experience.

One morning, my husband, Jeff, left the house for work, and headed up the street to get our car out of the garage, which was three blocks away.

Don't ask me to explain why our car was three blocks away. That is long story detailing the pitfalls of living in a city where real estate and parking are more precious than blood, and people will rent out every legal inch of their properties. Our previous landlord even leased a two-by-eight foot section of the garage under our house (where we could not afford to park) to some guy who kept his motorcycle there. I have no idea where the man lived, but every Saturday morning he woke up our entire building with the chugging of his Harley.

Anyway, Jeff was four houses up the block, on the way to the car, when he saw what looked like a cloth diaper on the ground.

"Hmm. That's interesting," he thought. "Maybe another family on the block uses cloth diapers." He shrugged and walked on.

Then he saw another. Then another. Then a whole pile of soggy, poopy messes that uncannily resembled our dirty diapers. He sprinted back to the house for a pair of surgical gloves. (They were left over from a box of hospital contraband that he swiped when Grace was newborn and he still endured squeamishness at changing her poops.)

Jeff tugged on the gloves, grabbed an extra plastic bag, and scurried back up the sidewalk, collecting rotten diapers as he went.

When I called the diaper service later that day, sure enough, there were no diapers on our porch that morning. Apparently, someone stole the bulging bag from our stoop, discovered its contents, and abandoned the foul-smelling loot in front of the neighbor's driveway.

I wondered what the thief thought he or she was getting? What could possibly entice someone to make off with and open a smelly blue plastic bag that sat on another person's porch?

It may relate to a San Francisco phenomenon that we call "the ultimate recycling." When people here get bored with the latest residuals of our consumer-hungry culture, and they are too lazy to sell it on eBay or give it to a charity, they just put it at the curb. If you leave a ratty ottoman outside your house at 8 p.m., there is a 96% chance that you will not see this item when your alarm buzzes the following morning. Some enterprising person will have snatched up your trash for their treasure.

We have benefited from such ground-scores. Jeff once snagged a pair of snow skis and a rotted artist's canvas, each slightly damaged, but suitable for creative re-use.

Maybe the would-be diaper thief thought he pilfered something that we genuinely left out for the taking. But maybe she sneakily, willfully, and deliberately seized an opportunity to steal another person's property.

No matter what motivation went down, it was a classic case of instant karma. Some goon thought he scored a sweet deal on our porch and literally got a sack of poop.

Starbucks Birthday Party

Birthday expectations get lowered when one becomes a parent.

When I turned twenty-two, my college roommates went berserk and threw me a huge surprise party. Our flat overflowed with about seventy of my closest friends, all jostling to make a big fuss over me. (And I desperately needed the attention.) Bouquets of fresh flowers jazzed up our hand-me-down end tables and sarcastic hand-lettered posters poked fun of the birthday girl from various zany locations. With all of the unbridled libido and hyperactivity of your typical red-blooded American, liberal arts majors, we devoured a giant cake and a floated a keg of Shiner Bock in about forty-seven minutes. I loved it.

What a difference a decade makes.

When I turned thirty-two, I met a gang of mama friends at the Starbucks on 24th Street the night before my birthday to discuss plans for a childcare co-operative. We didn't mean for it to be an impromptu celebration of my existence, but it was the best I could hope for at this juncture.

There were many reasons why I couldn't party like it was 1999, and instead celebrated with a more sedate gathering. My family's finances (or lack thereof) provided enough babysitting cash to hire either an escaped convict or a financially unsophisticated golden retriever. This situation long ago booted us out of the realm of decent affordable nighttime childcare.

Grandparents were too far away to come over and help out while Mama and Daddy dined someplace fancy. We didn't have enough old friends in San Francisco to throw me a shindig. Those who had the intentions sure as heck didn't have the time—too busy wrangling kiddos, work, and chaos of their own

(And who wants to get drunk these days anyway? No matter what time I go to bed, my daughter, Grace, will still start hitting me in the face at 6:30 a.m., yelling, "MOMMY, get up! No get up, Daddy! MOOOOOmmy! Get UP NOW!")

With this in mind, I interrupted our co-op discussion on the appropriate filling for the toddlers' organic, whole wheat, hormone-free sandwiches to declare our corporate coffeehouse gathering as my official birthday party. A Starbucks bash! Almost as cool as having your 10 year-old fete at McDonald's, except the coffeeshop party seemed a trifle more pathetic.

I put aside the lack of hipness of it all and focused on the inherent joy in being out of the house at after dark, during a time when I usually fold a month's worth of underwear or pass out in front of hubby Jeff's TiVo-ed University of Texas basketball games. Empowered by my proclamation, I sat back and silently congratulated myself on doing what all the mama self-help books say by "taking care of me."

We had no cake, nor keg. No witty limericks on the bathroom walls paid homage to my very being, yet I felt as much gaiety as I did ten years prior. Just being out in the world after 6:30 p.m. thrilled me to no end. The stale decaf and crusty, end-of-the-day baked goods evoked much more satisfaction and joy than say, the fourth cup of flat Schlitz on an empty collegiate stomach.

I think that as we cross the border into Grown-up Land and accumulate our many ensuing responsibilities, we more deeply appreciate the few snatches of adults-only fun that we can gather. In college, I frolicked all day long, taking time in between parties and sorority business to attend class or work at my 15-hour a week job. I was lucky. True obligations were few and far between.

But I am lucky now, too, I thought, and smiled across the table at the funky, clever mamas with whom I spend a great deal of my time.

Starbucks kicked us out at 10:00, but the night was young. It was way too early to go home to sleeping tots and computer-zombie spouses. No one wanted our big night out to end, but two of my partners in nightlife were pregnant and another one was nursing a six-month-old. We weren't exactly martini material.

So we stood outside of Starbucks for two hours and babbled at each other, jumping around to stay warm and comfortable on tired mama feet. Finally, a delivery truck pulled up and the stink of its exhaust drove us away. If not for that truck we might still be out there, celebrating the simple joy of being out with other adults after the sun goes down.

I can't complain about what may sound like a lame night out to the seasoned bar-hopper. In my book, my impromptu whoopty-do at the

Starbucks may not have been a high falutin' soiree, but it rivaled many a college kegger for mama's mood elevation.

At the end of the evening I shuffled up Sanchez Street, sober and alert, craning my neck to gaze at the starry sky with gratitude and amazement. A deep sense of serenity washed over me, like I had just found one of my post-cesarean section Vicodins. Seriously, it felt good to realize that at this point in my life I need a lot less fussing over, that I can find a calm satisfaction in the many rich blessings of my life: Good home, good family, good friends.

I crept in the front door to see Jeff hunched over the laptop, doing his part to keep us financially afloat in a city where one month's rent could feed a family in Pakistan for a year. Grace snoozed peacefully in her bed, her cherubic lips pouted and rosy cheeks puffed out, just like when she was a newborn.

Nah, I thought, I guess I don't have lowered expectations for my birthday. I just already have everything I need.

Who's Your Daddy?

When I look back at some of my old writing, I realize that my husband, Jeff, has been portrayed in a less than flattering light.

He has been described as a technology-addicted, TiVo-clicking, remote control-hogging, Napster-downloading, gangsta rap-loving, beer-drinking, middle-of-the-night-email-checking, comic book-reading, holey-underwear-wearing, jam band/garage rock/classic rock/new wave/alternative/any kind of music-obsessed, Howard Stern-listening, Mother's Day-ignoring, money-bungling, birthday-dismissing, absent-minded, sex-crazed, overgrown fratboy-college professor. (Message to Metallica: the Napster comment? Total joke. Please don't sue us.)

All of you women readers are probably rolling your eyes at his resemblance to some current or former man in your life.

All of you dude readers are probably going, so what's the problem?

The problem is that Jeff, as a child development professor who makes a career on advocating the value and significance of fathers in the lives of children, sometimes gets a little miffed at the constant cultural dismissal of daddies.

Oops.

Even though my stuff is (supposed to be) just for wacky laffs, I, too, am guilty of lampooning my child's papa in the name of a cheap chuckle. I'm just as bad as our mainstream entertainment outlets. Movies and TV too often characterize dads as clueless oafs, desperate for golf or beer, and trying in vain to get laid by mom. Flip on your favorite network sitcom on any given night of "family" programming to see what I mean.

Side note: what is up with all the hot moms and grody dads on TV? What real life mothers of small children actually look as fine as the women on *Everybody Loves Raymond* and that Jim Belushi show? Especially while cleaning up after those bozos. Has this question been done to death by the stand up comedians? I have no idea as I never go out anymore and I am usually passed out cold long before Letterman.

Anyway, as an apology to Jeff, and to all the papas everywhere who parent their kiddos with love and skill, (that's right, they PARENT...they don't "baby-sit" their own children) here is a bit of homage to some good fathering.

Reasons why Jeff is great:

Jeff is having kids while still young and healthy enough to play and be active without sustaining serious bodily injury. For example, Jeff can engage in a spontaneous football game and not rip his stiff Achilles tendons in half. (Special shout-out to my dad on that one. No more football for you, Grandpa!)

He not only grants my frequent requests for a mama's night out, he practically shoves me out the door and locks it behind me, yelling, "Don't come back until the bars close, you hussy!" Although this may only be a smokescreen for a night of illicit Playstation toggling, *Smallville* watching, and music downloading, I take it at face value and appreciate the freedom.

He insists that I attend my annual Girls Gone Mild vacation with my college girlfriends.

So that we could save money on childcare, and also keep our precious baby near and dear to us, Jeff was Grace's primary care provider for two days a week when I worked part time. He took Grace to campus and let her drool on his office supplies while he advised panicked grad students on their thesis projects. He gave Power Point presentations with Grace in the sling. He also got very behind on work and spent many evenings and weekends playing catch up.

He is Grace's best bath-time buddy. Although I recently learned that he routinely forgets to wash her feet and other important body parts, Jeff always gets her hair squeaky clean. He has even worked up an elaborate game of "hairstylist," in which Jeff endlessly grooms our toddler's locks as if primping her for an evening at the Golden Globes.

When I try to give Jeff verbal props on his fathering, he usually brushes me off and refers to a quote from comedian, Chris Rock: "You're *supposed* to take care of your kids!"

Meaning that he doesn't think he deserves praise for his relationship with his daughter any more than he should get praised for going to work each day. Good point.

Beyond the parenting stuff and into our interpersonal realm, there are countless little things that show me how he places relationships with family above all else.

Once, he chivalrously defended my sense of humor when attending an alternative, trance-rave-DJ wedding reception for some work friends. Jeff returned from the soiree having learned an important lesson: Never wear an "I'm With Stupid" t-shirt to a party full of humorously challenged PhD's.

Nevermind that the other guests were dressed like "Burning Man" attendees in drag—think silver glitter KISS boots, pink beehive wigs and angel wings. Jeff's shirt was about as welcome as an obsessive graduate student with a restraining order. He spent the evening defending the ironic iron-on, saying, "Robin gave it to me! And I think it's funny!"

Jeff is also quick to forgive my many screw-ups, both in motherhood and in our relationship. Like the time he swallowed his anger at me knocking his precious yet-to-be-read comic book fanboy magazine into the toilet (pre-flush). A tough one in Jeff-Land, and therefore all the more meaningful.

And did I mention that he is a hottie?

So now when Jeff accuses me of making him sound like a cross between a Star Trek conventioneer and a clueless lodger who drifts in and out of our home for scrambled eggs and *Sports Center*, I can direct him to this article.

It's about time I describe him as a computer-repairing, mass culture-purveying, fine beverage consuming, giggle-inducing, hard-working, humor-defending, bill-paying, bath-giving, father-advocating, baby-wearing, knowledge-gobbling, kind-hearted, cute-bootied, tall and sexy, heck of Dad.

Life in the Stay-at-Home-Lane

My life has changed drastically since I have left the ranks of suited professionals who worry about things like quarterly losses. I now dwell in that cluttered, sticky zone where my worries center on a quarter getting lodged in a curious toddler's windpipe.

There have been a few other changes since I have enlisted in the army of stay-at-home-parents.

Of course, the biggest blow has been to ye olde pocketbook. As anyone who has ever had the pleasure of paying $30 to park for an afternoon at Fisherman's Wharf knows, San Francisco is one pricey city.

Hoarding cash for luxuries, like bananas and baby wipes, means that I have reduced my clothing budget from $200 per month to $200 per year. I now buy clothes in bulk by going to Old Navy twice annually.

Each summer I buy ten long sleeved, $10 t-shirts in a variety of colors. By the winter, these shirts have become stained with poop, vomit, or some unidentifiable food shmear. So I go back to Old Navy and buy ten short-sleeved, $10 shirts. (No, I did not get my seasons confused. Remember, in San Francisco they are reversed.)

Now that I spend my days inside my own overpriced, rented house, I have become a born again artsy crafty person.

Inspired by the familiar walls and ratty furniture that my eyeballs swear to me they are sick and tired of seeing, I have enlisted the help of several hot carpenters from *Trading Spaces*. At least that is my excuse for indulging in my own desperate housewife equivalent of a Fabio novel by TiVo-ing every TLC home improvement show I can find.

Sometimes I don't shower until 2:00 p.m. Not because I spend the morning lounging about, sipping a mocha latte and watching a shirtless televised hunk build a spice rack. I am unwashed because I am busy playing chef, laundress, nurse, maid, chauffer, emcee and sherpa to a certain small, loveable person (i.e. my daughter, Grace).

I don't mind staying smelly. Most mornings I only see other parents in similar states of unwash, ferrying their own small, loveable people.

Another change: Sometimes I am lonely. I'll admit that I get more than a little tweaked for mature conversation. I desperately pounce on the other poor adults at the playground. And I can often be found yelling like a maniac over the back fence, annoying our leisurely, childless neighbors who spend their afternoons sunbathing. I'll talk to the mail carrier, the UPS man, and the nutjob dogwalker who drags sixteen slobbering pooches up and down Sanchez Street.

Now that I have left my part-time office job and I am wandering around the house full-time, I see a side of the City that most white-collar stiffs miss while they are tucked away in their cubicles. Who else is out and about? Other moms and a few dads. (In case you are wondering, the hot dads are usually in the Castro.)

I see garbage collectors. Construction workers. People who have green hair and alternative lifestyles and wake up at noon for coffee. Grad students. Work at home yuppies who take breaks to powerwalk with their iPods.

I have the dirt on the nanny mafia that rules my neighborhood park. I know which caregivers are warm, attentive saints who guard over their appointees better than the Secret Service. And I know which nannies spend their days gossiping in the shaded corners of the playground. Their wards dangle from the top of the jungle gym by one finger, or else scream it out, hysterical and abandoned, from strollers parked thirty yards away.

At the end of the workday, Grace and I often take a short walk to the end of our block. We sit on a bench and watch the J-Church train unload its chattel. Grace always posits the same intellectual query.

"What man doing? What woman doing?"

They are going home from work, usually wearing an urban version of business casual. Sleek black clothes, boots or trendy lace-up bowling shoes, a messenger bag, a funky scarf knotted about the neck.

Grace and I are wearing t-shirts, hoodies and sneakers that sport more colors than the Pride flag billowing over the Castro bus stop. A froggy backpack dangles from my weary shoulders. We are covered in dirt, almond butter, and crusty yogurt. We usually stink.

We sit on the bench on Church Street and admire the hurried pedestrians, busy on their cell phones or Blackberries.

Oh yeah, I don't use a Blackberry. And the cell phone is to call Daddy from the park to see when he will get home so we know when to make dinner.

Even though it can be tough, I am glad I spend my days hanging around the house. Life in the stay-at-home lane is good.

How to Raise a Texan in San Francisco

I've got integration on my mind these days. No, not the type where some disadvantaged kids are bussed into a rich white neighborhood to make them all go to school together. I'm talking about integrating the culture of my home state with my adult world. This has become especially relevant as I figure out how to parent my daughter, Grace.

Midland, Texas has a sign at its city limits proudly announcing that it is the hometown of George W. and Laura Bush. Every time I go home to visit my folks, this sign taunts me. It reminds me of the vast chasm between the city of my childhood and my adopted city of San Francisco, where most people think Bush is the devil incarnate.

The differences in my home state and my adult home have become even more apparent now that I am a mama. I love my West Texas roots, but I also thrive in the land of funky San Francisco chaos. I love Pride parades, Chinese grocery stores, D.I.Y. zine shops, and organic farmers markets.

This contrasts sharply with the land of my birth and upbringing.

Breastfeeding, the world's oldest form of infant nutrition, is still catching on in some pockets of Texas. The many young mamas who bravely nurse their babes in public often face judgment and shaming from old school idiots. Conversely, if you give a baby a bottle in a public place in San Francisco, you will probably have some well-meaning busybody come up and scold you for not using your God-given boobies to feed the child.

Out here we have gay mommies and daddies getting married. Back in my Texas high school (named for General Robert E. Lee) my gay friends got punched in the face quite regularly.

So I have a bit of resolving to do. I love the tolerance and diversity that surrounds my family in San Francisco, and I don't want to let go of my Texas heritage so much that I lose the good stuff.

How do I integrate it? How do I raise a Texan in San Francisco?

There are some subtle things. I make sure my daughter loads up on my dad's homemade Texas chili every Christmas. I play Willie Nelson lullabies when soothing my melted-down wee one. I wear my authentic Stetson straw cowboy hat to the anti-war rally.

I proudly wear the label of Texan. Many of my friends give me a regular shaming regarding the buffoon in the White House who emerged from my home state and hometown. I often humbly acquiesce, but not without offering an annoying lecture about all of the cool, smart people who are also from Texas.

Hell, yeah, I am from Texas! I love my boots, my country music roots and my Texas outspoken women heroes. I'm gonna teach my daughter about Molly Ivans, Ann Richards, Janis Joplin, the Dixie Chicks, and other loudmouth Texas women who have refused to let anyone squash their fiery spirits.

Grace is going to know her delightful Texas grandparents inside and out. From them she will learn about family, about sitting on a porch by a lake at sunset, about making homemade ice cream, about floating on inner tubes down curving Texas rivers. They will show her the subtle but important distinction between East Texas and West Texas barbeque sauce, how to dance the two-step, and where to explore the best fields of Texas wildflowers.

They will teach her compassion, like the kind demonstrated by my activist father-in-law, who made a millennial New Year's resolution to make a difference in the lives of Houston's children. They will share their intellect, like my mother-in-law, who single-handedly drives the Dallas chapter of the Association of University Women. They will pass on their creativity, the kind found in the traditional handcrafted needlework and sewing produced by my own Texas-grown mom.

Grace's Texas grandparents, people all as tactful and chivalrous as my own Daddy, will teach her the timeless southern art of graciousness and manners. From these wise elders she will gather her yes ma'ams and no sirs. She will acquire the unique driving salute, constantly observed on two-lane Lone Star highways, that we call the "Texas Friendly" wave.

It's my hope that she will take the best elements from the state of her parents' blood and use them to someday rock San Francisco. This city has quite a few loudmouths, but it could always use another loudmouth Texas woman.

Boogie Nights

I've done my share of dancing.

I writhed with adolescent pretension to the thumps of New Order at "teen nite" in a sleazy West Texas nightclub.

I drunkenly forced my husband to sweat it out with me in a gay bar in New York's Lower East Side at 3:00 a.m. We got our groove on to the likes of Queen, Madonna, and the queer classic, *It's Raining Men*.

I've tag-teamed with my college girlfriends as we busted dance moves while fighting off over-cologned, over-hairy creeps in an over-hyped, over-priced Vegas nightclub.

But nothing can top our all-family kitchen boogie sessions.

Admit it. We've all danced alone when we think no one is watching. Everyone has some embarrassing band, like Duran Duran or Big Country, that makes us want to shake our cabooses each time it pops up on the ol' classic rock dial.

Kids just give us an excuse to do it more freely. To give up all inhibitions and go nuts, without hiding from any potential onlookers.

I find that our family dance marathons occur most frequently when the most un-childlike music comes on our favorite local radio station, KFOG. We often get the Led out to Zeppelin's *Stairway to Heaven*, and I have been known to scream, "I come from a land down under!" at full throttle while bouncing along to Men at Work.

Speaking of bouncing, another fave is to enlist my hubby's jam band library and act out the lyrics to Phish's *Bouncing 'Round the Room*.

We're teaching our tot to do the Hustle and the Electric Slide. I can mimic the dances from *Saturday Night Fever* and Michael Jackson's *Beat It* video with eerie synchronicity. My hubby and I pretend to waltz and two-step to old country ballads that remind us of our Texas childhoods.

My kitchen floor has even seen its share of Mom's poppin' and breakin' moves, complete with my geriatric attempt at doing the Centipede. I am no candidate for an *Electric Boogaloo* film, but I can hold my own on the linoleum.

But the best times involve no funkadelic moves. Just a free-form, jumping, twirling, whirling dervish bit. It keeps me fit and ready for any competitions on one of those *Dance Dance Revolution* videogames that swept Japan a couple of years ago.

I am also doing a darn tootin' good job of turning my daughter off of any cool 80s dance music she might otherwise discover as retro and hip when she turns fourteen. If any of her pals try to turn her on to an old Cure album, her embarrassing memories of parental new wave dance sessions will make Robert Smith seem about as cool as Paul Anka.

So, if you peek in my window some evening, don't call 911. I'm not having a full body seizure as part of an allergic reaction to shellfish. I'm just doing my part to keep my family's Soul Train on track.

Losing It

I finally lost it.

Not my virginity. Obviously. Not my last remaining pair of cheapo Target sunglasses. Thank God.

I lost my nap. Rather, my daughter's nap. Meaning that I've lost my tiny window of mama-only time, a time usually devoted to reading, writing, or resting. If I'm not careful, I will also lose my...

Let's just say that I'm working hard not to lose my marbles.

Once upon a time, I held my helpless, sleepy newborn in my arms while she burned hours of daylight with her breastmilk-fueled nap marathons. I watched movies, read magazines, and surfed the web, never once believing the rumors that those idyllic times would come to an end. Like the first day of school, getting her driver's license, or going away to college, certain developmental landmarks of my daughter's growth were on the distant horizon, but I couldn't imagine that they were any more than myths to frighten new parents.

But this one is no myth. Grace, my former saint of daytime REM sleep, no longer takes a nap. My baby is a Big Girl now. Hence my lack of "me time" in the afternoon. Hence the delay (for those of you who take notice) in the timeliness of this column. Hence my feeling at the end of my (twelve to fourteen hour) work day that I have been run over by a twenty-seven-pound, two-year-old, almond-butter-munching steamroller.

The books say it's normal. Toddlers often stop napping around this age, and the average amount of sleep needed by a two-year-old is between nine and thirteen hours. My kiddo cuts logs for twelve hours at a stretch, so she's plenty rested. The problem is that she hits the pillow during the nighttime only.

This transition has left me with more fear and loathing than a gonzo journalist at a Las Vegas police officers' convention. Without my mama-time, I'm no good. I'm a lame parent, a sad sack of a spouse, and a generally miserable waste of biological material.

To combat this anxiety and exhaustion, I have begun to draw upon creative rest and rejuvenation techniques not used since college. Don't tell the experts, but I also compromise some of my highfalutin' parenting ideals so that I may keep my sanity.

Here are some of the ways my days have changed, now that I have finally lost it.

Television, once a terrifying no-no, is now switched on at least once a day. I am learning the names of all the new characters on Sesame Street who have been added since I was a kid. I don't mind. At least I can sit down for twenty minutes while Grace ogles Elmo.

Backyard play is much less structured and supervised these days. Sure I go out there with her, so that I can slump in a lawn chair and work a crossword. Meanwhile, my toddler romps barefooted across scratchy non-kid-friendly landscaping and tangles herself in decade's worth of spiderwebs.

Sometimes, when I really need to just collapse on the living room floor for a few seconds, I will let my daughter play alone in her room. I emerge each time, refreshed from my blackout, to discover a brand of carnage that can only be unleashed by an unsupervised toddler.

Imagine hundreds of diaper wipes emptied onto a suspiciously damp bed, drawers of clothes dumped out on the floor, an entire tube of lotion squirted atop a tidy line of stuffed animals, and one very naked child squealing in the middle of this mess.

I have also modified my writing technique. Right now I am writing this column by hand, sitting on my bed, at 3:30 in the afternoon, a time when Grace used to nap. She is playing on the bed with me, lovingly tucking her Baby Chou Chou under Mama's covers.

I must surreptitiously scribble these deeply insightful pronouncements in my Super Friends notebook while I perch in our laughably tiny, San Francisco-sized "master" bedroom and Grace romps in her Big Girl underwear. Using the computer is out of the question while this Big Girl is awake. That is, unless I guiltily shove her in front of another TiVo-ed episode of Elmo, risking increased loss of IQ points and future National Merit Scholar status.

This is all temporary. I know. Soon enough she will be in preschool and I will have oodles of hours in which to convince myself that my unique sentence structures do indeed make me the next Anne Lamott. But until then, I must creatively devour the precious few snatches of non-toddler time I can gather each day. Or else I may lose it.

And I don't mean my extra set of car keys.

Summers of 1985 and 2005:
Then and Now

Then I ate hamburgers from the grill, Ruffles potato chips and homemade ice cream cranked out in the kitchen sink. Now I eat pizza with whole-wheat crust, stir fry tofu and Ben and Jerry's Cherry Garcia ice cream.

Then I drank Big Red, orange juice, skim milk and Diet Coke. Now I drink coffee, dark beer, soy milk and Diet Coke.

Then I listened to Van Halen, Huey Lewis and Duran Duran. Now I listen to The White Stripes, The Killers and Duran Duran.

Then I watched *You Can't Do That on Television*, *Family Ties*, and *Who's the Boss*. Now I watch *Lost*, *The Office*, and way too many reality shows on TLC.

Then I put Tom Cruise on my top ten list of hotties. Now I want him to shut up with his bizarre judgments against Brooke Shields and leave moms alone.

Then I did my best to emulate Molly Ringwald, with my many layers of faux-thrift store, shoulder-padded clothing and high-top Converse sneakers. Now I do my best to emulate a human being, by showering daily and wearing clean underwear. And my daughter wears high-top Converse.

Then my best friend had long blond hair and parents who never enforced rules. I liked her because she was popular. Now my best friend has a receding hairline and he regularly enforces our family rules. I like him because he makes me laugh.

Then my mom nagged me to clean up my room. Now I wish I could keep my house as nice as my mother's.

Then my sister was always around, absconding with my latest Rick Springfield poster or Def Leppard cassette. I screamed at her to "just leave me alone!" Now my sister lives in New York City, neither of us can afford to go visit the other, and I wish we could hang out more often.

Then I rolled my eyes at my dad's often embellished, often repeated family stories. How many times could a girl hear the one about her dad being the first kid in his hometown to both survive a ninja attack and invent cold fusion? Now I am grateful I inherited his gift for storytelling. I still roll my eyes at his old goodies, and I am working on a few of my own.

Then summer meant long, sweaty Texas days, risking heat stroke and sunburn to tear it up in our cul-de-sac with a hoard of neighborhood kids. Now summer means long, foggy San Francisco days, tearing it up in a neighborhood park with a hoard of toddlers.

Then I traveled to New Braunfels, Texas to float in inner tubes down the river with my cousins. Now I travel from California to Texas twice a year, each time packing my social calendar more full than a Southwest Airlines flight to Vegas.

Then my Girl Scout troop saluted the flag when Vice-President George Bush came to town. Now I marched in an anti-war rally before President George Bush invaded Iraq.

Then I lived in a giant four-bedroom house with a swimming pool. My parents designed and built it. Now I live in a tiny ancient cottage that has survived numerous earthquakes and lord knows how many inhabitants.

Then I played Marco Polo in our backyard pool all day, leaving the water only long enough for lunch and the mandatory, twenty-minute, post-meal cramp prevention. Yes, I did pee in the pool. Now I take my daughter to swim class once a week in an indoor heated pool. Yes, she now pees in the pool too (and my husband has witnessed worse). But at least she wears a swim diaper.

Then I thought of junior high boys as sometimes-boogery messes and sometimes-interesting mysteries. Now I think of junior high boys as boogery messes who hog the baby swings at the playground. Go to the mall for cryin' out loud!

Then I thought of men as daddies. Now I have come full circle and I think of men as, well, daddies.

Then I wanted to hide behind my hair, so that no one would notice me. Now I want to hide behind my down comforter so that no one will make me vacuum up the stale cat hairballs that have fermented behind the sofa for the last eighteen months.

Then I teetered on the border between childhood and adolescence as I waited to enter junior high. I rode my bicycle around dusty West Texas fields all day and played with cosmetics once the sun went down. Now I teeter on a new border, walking that tightrope shared by many who attempt to maintain a sense of self in the face of parenthood.

Then I never worked out, but had plenty of exercise with all of that swimming, bicycling and general running around like an idiot. Now I never work out, but I get plenty of exercise pushing a stroller or carrying my daughter up and down San Francisco hills all day. And I still run around like an idiot.

Then I felt ugly, so I overcompensated with ridiculous makeup and 80s new wave, over-sprayed hair. Now I know I am not perfect but I have finally figured out how to accentuate my good features. (Important lessons of the 80s: Purple eye shadow = the bruised look. Hair-sprayed bangs up to the ceiling = fire hazard.)

Then I was twelve. I waited to become an adult, where I thought the universe would magically unfold and offer up all of its answers. Now I am thirty-two. Will someone please call me when this unfolding occurs? I don't want to miss it.

Girls Gone Mild

I just got back from my annual Girls Gone Mild vacation.

That's right. It was MILD. I did not miss a keystroke there.

Every summer, my college girlfriends and I hook up for a vacation weekend away from families, work and responsibilities. And to the hormonal thrill seeker, our gig may sound a bit boring.

We do not take body shots off a hot bartender. We do not flash our boobs in a tacky ploy to redeem microscopic self-esteem. We do not wake up in a puddle of our own vomit, wondering how to best escape a seedy Florida hotel room without being spotted doing the Walk of Shame.

Instead, we laugh, cry, drink wine, and indulge in luxuries such as spa treatments. Our generally tame festivities caused a snickering spouse, who shall remain nameless, to call it like it is, and offer up the Girls Gone Mild moniker.

And it stuck.

This year's Mildness served its intended purpose of rest and rejuvenation, with an added eye-opener. While traveling with three of my most appealing lady friends, I had the epiphany that I have been virtually invisible for a couple of years. At least to strangers of the opposite sex.

As four attractive (if I say so myself) thirty-something women, without men or children, we got a lot of head turns and once-overs with the ol' sneaky eyeballs. In fact, if I may use the lingo of the kids these days, I would say that we regularly got checked out.

Maybe I looked better than usual. After all, I was sporting the combination of styled hair, a kicky skirt and well-applied makeup. Most days I consider myself sexy if I leave the house boasting just one of those accoutrements.

But I think it was more than that. I think I got critically reviewed because I was without a man or a child.

Most of the time when I am out in public, I am with my two-year-old daughter. She generally acts as a human shield, deflecting all hints of sexuality off of her tired mama.

It's true. Society dictates that mommies aren't to be ogled. Or as one of my cruder friends so indelicately put it, we are now in the category of the "unscrewable." Don't get me wrong. I am not trying to stir up a little something outside the bonds of my happy marriage. But I freely own up to my vanity, and I like to think that I look good when I am out and about in the world.

So it was a surprise to me when men (albeit paunchy, hairy, leering men) actually checked me and my girlfriends out.

It all started in the airport.

Maybe the leerers were only drawn to my sex-kitten-Amazonian-best-buddy, or maybe I had delusions of grandeur. However, I do believe that the dudes looked all of us up and down, not just the tall, voluptuous one. We were all minimally in the "cute" category, and we were dolled up in our Girls Gone Mild freedom attire.

Once we got to Happy Hour I started to get the hang of all the once-overs. Like the drunk freak who wouldn't leave us alone. He said he shared his hotel room with Ron Howard and kept inviting us up to meet Opie.

Of course, no one was interested—a gal's gotta be pretty darn desperate to believe that Ritchie Cunningham can't afford his own suite and needs to shack up with a porcelain salesman from Albuquerque. But I was flattered, nonetheless.

By the time the weekend wound down and we all waited back at the airport for our separate flights across the country, getting cruised had become downright ho-hum.

Whatever. Yea, that dude is watching us. Being stared at is so boring.

It made me think about how women cannot be both mamas and magnetic. Most of the time, we're too busy trying to stay awake and keep the yogurt out of our hair to worry about looking like cast members of *The OC*. And when we do actually truss up, the pheromone-repellent presence of our offspring rebuffs potential admirers.

So, it gave me a shot in the arm to get a few looks. Even if the givers of said looks might only have been considering me the sad side-dish next to my main-course, model-esque gal pals. Heck, at this stage, I'll take what I can get.

When I returned from the trip, I told my hubby about my too-obvious realization that moms are not the sex bombs. He agreed that even cutie mamas give off a non-foxy vibe.

"When guys check out a mom, she is usually compromised in some unflattering position," he said. "She is bending over a stroller or squatting in some freakish way. Checking out a mom is kind of like looking at a cadaver. It is for research purposes only."

Thanks, hon.

He also said that I am still super hot in his eyes. Which is all I really needed to know.

Although I enjoyed basking in an unusual amount of male attention while I got Mild with my girls, it was great to get back to my most important admirer.

Ogling truly begins at home.

Burn the Man!

"Thank you, Burning Man, for taking away your followers for the weekend!"

So read the hand-lettered sign in the apartment window at the intersection of Divisadero and Haight Streets.

Our City by the Bay was eerily free of freaks, except for the truly freaky street kids who didn't have the cash to pony up for Burning Man admission. It was kind of like after the Rapture in those creepy *Left Behind* books, where only the unsaved get to stay behind when God swoops all the faithful up to heaven. Except we had only the uncool left behind in San Francisco.

"I kind of agree with that sign," Jeff gestured up to the window of the shabby Victorian. I meekly nodded at my husband, hoping that no cash-strapped Burning Man devotee would overhear us and plot a trance-music and body-paint fueled revenge.

At the risk of alienating many of my urban friends and setting myself up as the complete and total square that I am, I have to say, I really don't get the Burning Man thing.

I'm open-minded. I know that the event started out as art and has evolved somewhat into drug-fueled commercialism. But I think that I need to actually attend to make sense of the Burning Man experience.

I hate to dredge up the details of Burning Man for those who know all about it, but in case you don't, here is a quick and dirty definition. Burning Man is described on its official web site (www.burningman.com) as "an experimental community, which challenges its members to express themselves and rely on themselves to a degree that is not normally encountered in one's day-to-day life." This weeklong temporary village springs up in the blistering Utah desert once a year and it has no rules or codes of conduct. Attendees must pack in all of their food and supplies, and the only things for sale are coffee and ice.

Participants wear daring wigs, incredible costumes and displays of nudity not seen since Woodstock. Days of freeform art, music and art-car parades culminate in a giant party where a monstrous effigy of "the Man" is spectacularly burned. During this bonfire, onlookers shake their dreds, bang drums, and wave glowsticks while chanting, "Burn the Man! Burn the Man!"

Who is "the Man?" In keeping with the free-for-all nature of the event, that definition is up for interpretation. For the cerebral, he is our material culture, our patriarchal rule, our anger at the destruction of the environment, our repressive ethics, yadda yadda yadda. He is George Bush, Donald Trump or Alan Greenspan. For the wasted, he is just really freakin' cool, dude.

Every fall Jeff complains about his academic colleagues who sneakily cancel classes to attend this week of debauchery in the desert. He has to cover for them so that the old fart faculty don't find out that several young professors are blissing out in Utah instead of teaching psychology to impressionable young minds.

Don't get me wrong. Jeff's university has a bit of a psychedelic history. Ken Kessey ran acid experiments on campus in the sixties. Free-love faculty got it on in what is now the clinical psych lab of Jeff's straight-laced, republican colleague. Jerry Garcia jammed on the campus radio. Grace Slick and Big Brother and Holding Company once rocked campus as the homecoming band.

But the old-timey professors who stuck around after the love-ins of the sixties are more settled down these days. They own homes in wealthy Marin County, and their ponytails dangle below shiny bald domes. They don't get Burning Man, and neither do I. Why would I want to live in a trailer, in one hundred degree weather, for a week, with no shower and nothing to mask my body odor except patchouli and body glitter?

Remember that I write about Burning Man as a curious onlooker, one who has never braved the harsh sand and sun in the name of free-form artistic community. Maybe because I am a drama geek from West Texas, I had enough of heat and costumes as a teenager. Try wearing a Tweedle-dee suit in 90-degree Texas sunshine for an afternoon of children's theater and you will be cured of any Burning Man itches faster than you can say heat rash.

Maybe, because of my Burning Man virgin status, I just can't visualize the sense of one-ness, the pure energy of so many people coming together for the creation of a fleeting, creative society. Maybe it is time I open my mind and take a peek into the other side. Cross the border into the Black Rock Desert of Utah. Offer up the chant: BURN THE MAN! BURN THE MAN!

Lucky for me, they do have a kid section, where families stake out their campers and tents in a wild and wooly child-friendly zone. And the experience would probably enhance my writing.

I can just imagine taking my daughter, Grace, to the Utah desert to dance in butterfly wings and a purple wig while swinging sparklers and riding a truck decorated like a hippopotamus. No baths for a week and more trippy-looking folks than the Haight-Ashbury Street Festival. My mother's nightmare comes to life.

Yes, perhaps I should go and Burn the Man—even thought it is about ten years past its prime. Then I will no longer be one of those who are Left Behind.

Private Parts

The paper mache butterfly project was supposed to represent the joy and celebration of summertime. It looked more like male genitalia.

And let me make the disclaimer that I use the term "paper mache" very lightly. The soggy conglomeration of water, flour and balloons rotted on the kitchen counter for over four hours before a single drop began to evaporate.

"Holy cow!" my husband gasped when he came in from work and saw the pornography on the linoleum.

"It's supposed to be a butterfly," I said.

"Good job, hon!" He laughed and reached past the obscenity for a cookie.

I'll admit that this latest crafty creation took my family one step further from the pages of *ReadyMade* magazine and one step closer into our official status as a house of ill-repute. Not that we had too far to fall.

My kid, Grace, already regularly barges into the bathroom as soon as she sees Mama sashay in to relieve herself. After forcing her way past the closed door she yells for anyone who has yet to learn that "Mommy has a vagina!"

Rather than call more attention to this delicate fact, I will calmly say, "Yes. I do." And make yet another mental note to buy a dang lock for our turn-of-the-century bathroom door.

This attention to body parts supersedes our family residence. Before stumbling home the other day to embark on our butterfly craft-fest gone awry, Grace and I spent the morning at the park. Desperate in her quest to practice using the potty at every infested commode in town, Grace insisted that she needed to go in the crusty john at the Upper Noe Rec Center. While I helped her to perch on the possibly infectious porcelain, she shared her knowledge of anatomy with our peers in the restroom.

"That boy have penis!" she yelled.

I nodded inconspicuously, hoping that, in our gender-bending city, the kid in question was indeed a little dude.

I think it may be time to have the "private parts" talk with my daughter, before she decides to pull one of her Michael-Jackson-video-style-naked-crotch-grabs in front of the neighbors.

Of course, as usual, I am probably overreacting. A fascination with body parts is a normal, healthy part of toddler development. And folks in my adopted city of San Francisco aren't exactly shy about letting it all hang out, so to speak.

So I bit the bullet and took the censorship-worthy paper mache with us to our childcare co-operative. I planned to duly impress our teacher with my uncanny knowledge of paper mache piñata construction. With a mix of pride and embarrassment I handed over the alleged "butterfly" for Teacher's inspection. She gently took the homemade phallus in her hands, and knelt at eye-level with Grace.

"It is beautiful," she said, with a solemn stare into my child's artistic eyes. Grace squealed with delight and hugged her piñata to her chest, nearly crushing the testicles, I mean wings.

I was humbled, shamefaced at my family's squalid attributions heaped upon a lovely product of toddler sweat and imagination. Leave it to our inspired teacher to remind me of the simple innocence of a child, to remind me that I should celebrate her artwork, not dwell on the fact that Mama's miscalculation of balloon placement caused it to look like something out of the pages of *Playgirl* magazine.

I need to get my mind out of the gutter, I thought.

Sometimes parents need a reminder of these basic truths. We need a nudge to assist us fouled and cynical adults in seeing the world through the eyes of childhood. Nothing is dirty or suggestive in a child's sweet little world. Everything is new, fresh and beautiful.

I stared into space, musing on these insights. Our teacher then looked up from her communion with Grace and gave me a knowing wink.

Turns out I wasn't the only mama with her mind in the gutter.

S'More Camping, Please!

We've started taking family camping trips.

They are joyous respites from the humdrum of everyday living and the shock of recent hurricane catastrophes. With no radio, TV or Internet, my little family can spend a few days under some towering redwood trees, forgetting about Katrina, the Supreme Court, work and bills.

Maybe escape is not the most socially responsible response to national tragedy, but a few days in the arms of Mother Nature works wonders for both parents and child. Camping in the wilderness helps me to return back home with a scaled-down approach to what I really need in this world and a fresh appreciation for my many true blessings.

And, like most experiences with a kid, roughing it with offspring offers indelible moments of adult education that you just can't find in a Sierra Club pamphlet.

A few lessons I learned from our most recent camping trip with a toddler:

Banana slugs actually look like bananas. Do not attempt to eat them.

If you see a mountain lion, very stealthily pick up your child without bending your knees. Do not crouch or kneel, as that will make you seem vulnerable—just magically gather the little person to your chest by lengthening your arms like Plasticman. Stare into the eyes of the beast. Raise your jacket over your head to appear larger. Flap your arms. Slowly back away without running or breaking eye contact. If you can accomplish all of these things and not get eaten, congratulations, you are either the Beast Master, the Blair Witch, or you have recently graduated from an expert level course in Kundalini Yoga.

People without small children go camping for a unique reason: to get drunk and holler in the woods. The combination of intoxicated yodeling and paper-thin tent walls can be very distressing to parents. (Thank goodness our kiddo sleeps like a hibernating opossum.)

To counterbalance any potential child-waking nighttime noise, make sure your child benefits from a full infusion of the camping experience by rising with or before the sun. Encourage her to loudly share her joie de vivre with your hung-over neighbors by singing her praises to the glorious morning.

Go ahead and convince yourself that you can control the whole morning thing. It's not like you can keep her quiet anyhow. (See below.)

The museum at the ranger station can have some confusing taxidermy. Especially if part of your family history involves the legend of a coyote eating off grandpa's toe. (In reality, he shot the dang thing off in a tomfoolery hunting accident, but that is a whole 'nother column.) Example: "That's a coyote! It ate Bob-O!" my daughter yells at the stuffed dog. The ranger looks up from her desk, startled. I smile and shuffle Grace along to the woodpecker exhibit.

A broken potty in the community bathroom evokes more toddler excitement than a thousand ancient redwoods, clear streams, or three-story waterfalls. Staring at strangers making feeble attempts to groom in the rusted bathroom mirror also provides hours of thrilling entertainment.

Hikes to and from the broken john can easily log ten times more miles than attempted forays into the California wilderness.

That warning about hiding your food from raccoons is no joke. A giant masked critter, weighing more than a two-year-old child, can smell traces of s'more on a toddler's breath as far as five miles upwind.

It may as well be Christmas morning when a toddler wakes up inside a tent. The thrill of the sleeping bag! The chill of the air! The stillness of a sleeping Daddy, just waiting for a leap onto the family jewels! It demands some serious screeching. Another example: "Good morning, Daddy! I SAID good MORNING little DADDY!!!" This is a favorite way to greet the dawn. I secretly smile from inside my cozy sleeping bag bundle. My inner bitch cackles at such excellent revenge on the drunken screaming sorority girls who whooped it up until 4:00 a.m. Karma sure stinks, doesn't it, ladies?

Cooking breakfast on a campfire, while a squealing kid dances around the flames in her longhandles, can be a recipe for disaster. Be sure to keep plenty of child-safe toys nearby—I find banana slugs and conked out toilets make excellent distractions. However, when appreciated at a respectful distance, campfires can be almost as entertaining as broke-down commodes.

These are but a few marshmallow-ed nuggets of camping insight. As we continue our brave family explorations into the wild, I will update you loyal readers as necessary. Meanwhile, I plan to share my list with the good folks at Sierra Club, in case they wish to make it into a helpful pamphlet.

Zoo-Lander

Holy cow, I recently took five two-year-olds to the zoo. And it was a little hectic.

Have you ever taken five two-year-olds anywhere? Besides the safe confines of your expertly childproofed living room? Then you know that it is like hosting five feral cats for their annual bath.

Thank goodness I was not the only adult present for this five-kidded romp at the San Francisco Zoo. Fortunately, our field trip also featured another mama who was a delegate from our childcare co-operative. If not for her presence I might have locked the children in with the meerkats until I could find a decent manure wagon in which to cart them all away.

As anyone who has taken even one excited child to the zoo knows, it can be a grueling experience for the adults involved. Five kids, while delightfully entertaining, ranked as high as climbing out of the Grand Canyon on my personal top ten list of activities that made me lose my body weight in sweat.

I think it was my presence that started our trip off on the wrong foot. At least that is the best answer I can come up with, since our other field trips, chaperoned by other mamas, had far less chaos. The reports from those excursions shared lovely tales of joy and discovery, sprinkled with butterfly wings and fairy dust.

Our trip, perhaps because of my presence or perhaps because it featured the petting zoo, had no such luck. It started out with one wily kid who broke the cardinal rule of the zoo visit, running away several times, prompting a forced sit-out at the carousel ride. After one breathless chase through the chicken coop, I asked her why she chose to run away so often. Like any intelligent two-year-old, she patiently explained to me that she was not running away. She was merely chasing her toy cat, which had done the actual running.

Another sweet little guy got extremely agitated at the pushy goats which kept ramming him at eye-level, thinking he had a pocket full of treats. I can't say I blame him. Who wants a stinky pack of horned yahoos bumping into your forehead all morning? I spent a lot of time carrying this frightened child around, hoping to soothe his fears enough to help him have a sort of decent time at the zoo.

Of course, when Mommy carries another kid, my little girl goes bonkers. This led to me hoisting one (heavy) toddler on each hip while simultaneously kicking back any aggressive goats that got too near the toddlers' toes. I felt like a pack mule soccer player.

After about an hour of this workout, my biceps ached from lifting thirty-pound kiddos, my toes throbbed from knocking on goat horns, my head pounded from constant exposure in the harsh sunshine, and my throat begged for a drink of water.

Let me stop right here and apologize if I sound negative about this whole thing. Taking a crew of tots to the zoo was, in truth, an enchanting experience. But it was one of those activities that a person has to humorously download or she'll spontaneously combust. And we did have a whole slew of those charming moments that can only be found in the company of wide-eyed little kids.

The funniest bit had to be at the end of our trip, away from all of the non-human animals. Due to unforeseen potty circumstances, we all arrived back at the cars one hour later than planned. In our haste to hustle the kids out of the zoo, we forgot to pay for our parking, which could only be done back inside the gates.

Quicker than you can say "hungry goat," we built our own temporary zoo in my Honda by corralling all five children inside the car while my fellow mama ran back to pay for the parking. The three kids who rode with me were already securely tied up, I mean safely *buckled* up, in the backseat.

But the other two tykes, whose driver momentarily abandoned us to ensure our ability to actually leave the zoo, romped freely about the front seat. I sat on the hood and wished that I had taken up smoking in my youth. Now seemed like a great time for a cigarette.

When we finally got all five children settled into both cars, I sank down in the driver's seat and started the engine.

Suddenly the car went nuttier than a loaf of vegan sandwich bread.

The windshield wipers swished at a thousand miles per hour. The air-conditioning screamed at full blast. The left turn signal blinked. The hazards flashed. The radio blared.

It scared the bejeezus out of me.

By this point exhaustion had won the battle and I may have been more than a little delirious. However, once I realized that my car was not possessed by Christina, but rather by the curious fingers of small children, I about busted a gut. It was the funniest thing that happened to me since the time my husband accidentally slipped on the same banana that I had dropped in front of my house earlier in the day. (Another story.)

The chorus of, "What? What funny? What Robin laughing at?" ringing from the backseat only served to intensify my guffawing. There is nothing like a couple of two-year-olds playing in the front seat of your car to help redeem a draining day at the zoo.

A Princess Story

"Nice job, feminist mommy!"

So said my buddy at the playground when I announced my daughter's final choice in Halloween attire.

It's a princess. Yes, a princess. An honest-to-God, blue chiffon wearing, puffy-sleeved, need-a-prince-to-slay-the-dragon-kill-my-evil-stepmother-kiss-me-out-of-this-stinkin'-coma princess.

After considering several thousand possibilities, including a mermaid, a giraffe, a pink leopard, macaroni and cheese, and Supergirl (my personal favorite) our two-year-old declared that she would be a princess.

My comic book-loving husband was also especially excited about the Supergirl possibility. He proposed that he and I delve into DC Comics geek lore and garb ourselves as Supergirl's cosmic parents from the planet Krypton. (Think Marlon Brando's groovy turtlenecked getup in the original *Superman* film.)

Alas, when my daughter, Grace, made her formal decree of princess-hood, we tossed the Superfamily idea right into the circular file, along with my prefab expectations for this year's Halloween. What's a feminist to do?

At first I couldn't fathom where she came up with such a retro girly-girl notion. We live in a progressive, culturally critical household, where my kid has yet to discover Cinderella and other pink plastic offshoots of Disney marketing blather.

For instance, when Grace was an infant someone gave her a University of Texas cheerleader Barbie. It gave me heebie jeebie flashbacks to a childhood full of confusing expectations, a time when I thought beauty meant to be (a) a cheerleader, (b) blonde, and/or (c) Barbie. We relegated the bizarrely proportioned doll to the UT knick-knack collection that decorates several shelves in my husband's office.

I have a long history of such subversion. I wrote my college honors thesis on women's history. I shun cartoons and children's books that promote negative and unhealthy gender stereotypes. I read *Sassy* magazine in high school and I have since graduated to *Ms.* I regularly go without makeup, and I let my legs stay unshaved for weeks at a time. (Although one may argue that the body hair is more a product of laziness and dull razors than any sort of desire to make a political statement on the subjugation of the female via the patriarchal cultural model designed to objectify women's bodies into hairless, ageless, flawless, pornographic tools to sell beer.)

Parenthood certainly makes me eat my words. As I admire Grace's iridescent, blue tulle princess costume, I cringe in remembrance of the highfalutin' women's studies classes and anthropology books I dove into as an earnest young undergraduate.

My twenty-year-old self solidly determined that no daughter of mine would dare play into the hands of vicious gender stereotypes. Such pigeonholing would only open the door to a lack of confidence in the classroom, eating disorders, letting men use her for sex, and who knows what other evils.

But Grace found out that she could be a princess for Halloween after a lengthy conversation with another two-and-a-half-year-old who also wants to be a princess for Halloween.

Did I mention that this friend is a boy?

How very San Francisco. My spouse, who catches the train to work in the Castro neighborhood of our fair city, reports on seeing male princesses several times a week.

Before I ever had a kid I declared that no emancipated daughter of mine would ever be a freakin' princess for Halloween. She would go as a non-gendered animal, a piece of organic produce or a famous woman in history, such as Golda Meir or Murphy Brown.

I also said a lot of things before I ever had a kid that later came back to bite me in the hiney, big time. I said that I would never use plastic toys. I would never let my baby sleep with me. I would never breastfeed my baby when she was old enough to ask for it by name. So, I guess I have gotten pretty used to going back on my once rock-solid dogmas.

As a parent, I still read books about raising a strong, independent girl in a society where women become commercialized sex kittens at a younger and younger age, and a woman's value is increasingly based on her ability to look perfect. Just check out any trashy tabloid or stalker blog on Lindsay Lohan or the Olsen twins if you don't know what I mean.

And yet, my little girl picks up the notion of being a princess from a little boy. That is my only respite from this cruel irony.

That, and the fact that she looks damn cute in her tiara.

Our frilly costumed episode may just be a new opportunity for this liberated mama to compromise gender ideals in the name of individualism. If my daughter pursues the life of a girly girl, complete with cheerleading and Barbies, perhaps I will have little choice but to bite the pink bullet and deal with it.

Of course, part of dealing with it will be an insistence that my girly girl has a strong sense of self. That she has enough confidence and sass to tell shallow society where to stick it when it comes to extreme makeovers and glass ceilings.

And now our family costumes have evolved from a gang of butt-kicking super heroes into a princess and her royal parents, with a small subversive detail. We plan to punk ourselves out and carry Jeff's guitars and Grace's toy keyboard, as official representatives of the Royal Family of Rock.

We will probably look more like the Partridge Family than the Sex Pistols, but I will gain solace in knowing that I am not a complete and utter slave to the helpless-without-a-prince empire of girlhood costuming.

And, secretly, I must admit that I will enjoy wearing my own tiara. I am trying to view it like a symbol of honor, some props for a job well done in raising a kid so far. Feminist mommies can wear crowns, can't they?

And who knows, my daughter may change her mind at the last minute and dig her giraffe suit out of the costume trunk. In which case I will have to scramble to find a coordinating adult getup that still works with my own tiara.

A Child's Garden of Eatin'

We just got back from a trip to New York City where we visited my hipper than hip sister, her screamingly cool husband, and my beautiful best friend from college. This vacation made me realize that, in addition to my travel-savvy daughter already hitting Hawaii, both coasts, and several states in-between before her third birthday, she has also surpassed her parents' culinary wisdom at quite a young age.

Allow me to clarify. My child regularly consumes many types of food that my husband and I had not heard of until we'd reached college or beyond. At this rate, by the time she reaches adulthood, she will be a world-class connoisseur with a championship palate on some futuristic intergalactic version of *Iron Chef*.

Beyond the traditional ethnic varieties of Mexican, Chinese and Italian fare, Grace has tasted Thai, Korean, French, Japanese, Vietnamese, Greek, Peruvian, Ethiopian, Cuban, Burmese, Indian, and Mediterranean dishes. Not only are these culinary selections a normal part of her dining experience, she regularly asks for specific meals by name.

Imagine a two-year-old, redheaded white girl yelling across the kitchen, "Do we have edamame, Mama?" or, "I want hummus and tabouli for lunch!"

I remember being a kid and thinking that a fortune cookie seemed exotic. Ginger was downright unheard of.

I know I am not alone when I compare field notes with my fellow urban parents. Many of us grew up eating nutritious, healthy, but not such worldly foods. Now that we are fancy schmancy adults and we enjoy the wide range of dining options in San Francisco, our kids are developing appetites more refined than those of Food Network junkies.

Grace loves to snack on almond butter or tofu. I ate Jif. And my weirdo husband still does. Her beverage of choice is vanilla-flavored soymilk. I relished 2% milk with chocolate Quik. My daughter squeals with delight when we go out for dim sum, and she regularly begs for a cup of decaf chai with honey and cream. I loved getting pizza and a coke.

As enablers to our daughter's budding love of diverse foods, we have been planning her first sushi experience since probably before birth. Her favorite kitchen toy is a deluxe Japanese food set, complete with maguro, hamachi and a host of sushi rolls I can't even name. The day she takes her first big girl bite of raw tuna will be a Kodak moment to share with the grandparents.

She also knows all about Mama's love of lattes, and constantly asks to taste one of my caffeine-drenched adult candies from the neighborhood coffee shop. I tell her that the coffee drink will have to wait a few years beyond her first taste of sushi.

Sometimes I wonder if my child's upscale dining preferences indicate a future of pretentious food snobbery, where she will snootily push away plain ol' casseroles in favor of expensive epicurean creations. Then I remember that she never eats fast food or drinks sodas and I throw my fears of food snobbing out the window. How can a health-conscious mama devote any real amount of worry to her daughter liking a variety of nutritious, if exotic, fare?

We don't buy super-sugar-rainbow-sprinkled-artificially-flavored-chemical-coated-nasty-puffs or anything with the word "frosted" in its name. She will discover all of that garbage on her own time, and if, meanwhile, she wants to turn up her nose to partially-hydrogenated landfill in favor of healthy Thai lemongrass noodles then it's fine with me.

Snobby or not, Grace's tastes in food are a source of constant amusement, and I often share my insight on her broad spectrum of nourishment with friends and family. When we were in New York and I babbled about these observations once again, my brother-in-law gave a wise bit of input.

"Our country has undergone a sort of cultural food revolution," he said. "Everyone eats more gourmet and ethnic foods, not just kids."

Ah yes. I thought. We are, after all, a nation that worships Martha, Wolfgang and that "Bam" guy from Louisiana. And any simple Google search reveals that the sales of items like Portobello mushrooms and imported olives have shot up in recent years. My kid just reflects the smorgasbord of yummy groceries that permeates the culture around us.

Even so, I can't help but laugh when it is time to snack on some cheese.

I usually get a request such as, "Do we have Brie?"

"No, we have yellow cheese."

"I no like yellow cheese. I like Brie."

"Sorry, we're out of Brie." Of course, secretly I am stashing the Brie to munch with some Merlot and crackers once Daddy gets home.

"Oh. Then do we have Gouda?"

Sheesh!

Judgment Day

My husband and I have an ugly vice. We tend to get a little judgmental. We know it is wrong. It is a weak cover up for our own insecurities. It is mean. It is not What Jesus Would Do. Yet we do it anyway. (And you know you do it too. But this time, I'll take the heat for all of us.)

Back when we lived in Arizona, we used to take road trips with another lovely, and sometimes judgey, couple. After a day of snow skiing and a few too many beers (this is pre-kids, mind you) we would sit back and congratulate ourselves on being so much better than everyone else.

"Can you believe the way that loser didn't return her cart at the grocery store?" one of us would say.

"Or how about the geek who drove with his right turn signal blinking all the way to Flagstaff?" another of us would counter-offer.

Then we would all laugh and make a toast to being a bunch of "Judgey Judgersteins." We were jerks and we knew it.

Then parenthood came along. And, as any well-meaning mommy or daddy knows, judgment descends on new parents like the wrath of Khan. Indeed, the tables turn and judgey types get their own karmic bite on the booty. No matter what you do as a parent, there is always someone standing by, ready to judge.

It's true, isn't it? Raise your hand if you felt the heat of judgment burning a hole in your worried little head each time you informed a new person of your decision to let your baby sleep with you/buy a giant new crib/wean your six-month-old early/keep breastfeeding past one year/go back to work/quit your job? You get the idea.

How do we parents retaliate? We judge right back. It keeps us safe. It reassures us that our decisions are valid and that we won't be growing our spawn into the next Charles Manson.

And it can get ugly.

My husband and I recently came back from an adult friend's birthday party and compared notes on how we both silently judged a woman's choice not to breastfeed. And then we learned that her baby was adopted. Guess who felt like the schmuckiest couple at the party?

This made me realize that we really don't know any bad parents. Everyone we know is a good parent. Everyone. So what if they use a stroller instead of a sling. So what if they buy their three-year-old too many annoying electronic, plastic, landfill toys. So what if they're waiting an extra year to start preschool or ditching the school gig altogether in favor of homeschooling. The fact that they'll sit and have a conversation about their parenting decisions means that they care and they are attentive. They are doing more than just meeting the basic needs of the little lives that depend on them.

And, let's face it. There are some seriously bad parents out there. I'll put aside the horror-show examples, the atrocities, and the abuses that we don't even want to think about. Even when we exclude parenting transgressions of the criminal variety there is still a second-level tier of plain old bad parents.

I saw such parenting mayhem when I recently watched a televised cerebral stimulant called *Nanny 911*. The show is on Fox, so even if you have never had the pleasure of watching this class act, you can probably lose a few brain cells just by imagining what it contains.

On this reality show, the parents were so overwhelmed by their three-year-old twins that they constantly blew off their five-year-old boy. At bedtime they stuck the boy in his bed, plugged in a movie and put the fear of all things evil in him should he dare to get up. The little guy was so eager to please (and so terrified) that he didn't dare leave his room to go to the bathroom. So he peed in a cup and hid it in a cabinet. When his mom discovered the mug o' urine she completely freaked out, screaming at him that he was disgusting. I visualized the poor kid at age thirty, recounting the ego-blasting "pee in the cabinet" story to his therapist.

Now that's some bad parenting. These folks weren't necessarily bad people, but there is no doubt that they needed some guidance. Even though it was cheesy and simplistic and terribly produced, thank goodness Fox was there to step in.

And, of course, I judged them.

And then I took a step back and considered all of the lovely families I know in real life. Families of various ethnic and national backgrounds. Families who speak different languages at home, go to different churches, don't go to church at all. Families who have no daddy at home or two mommies. Families with financial abundance and families who struggle each month to make ends meet.

And all of these families have one thing in common. They have good parents.

All of the blessed little children who are lucky enough to be born unto the many families we know are just that, blessed. They spend their days and nights surrounded by halos of adoration and gratitude, doted on by parents who know darn well the miracle of each unique sweet baby.

We are all good parents. Everyone I know. You too.

So next time you hear me judge someone for giving their two-year-old too much sugar or letting their four-year-old watch an extra hour of TV, don't call me Ms. Judgey Judgerstein. Just force me to watch a horribly produced reality TV show and then make me take a look around me.

I might decide to stop judging for a minute.

The Chil'ing of Modern Manners

"Take this shit back!"

The S-word bellowed over the noise of the televised football game, the tipsy chatter, and the piped-in Doobie Brothers music. I couldn't help but turn around and stare.

The too-classy-for-words object of my gaze was a pasty guy, probably around thirty. He wore a grubby white hat with a Texas sports logo that I have since forgotten, and a slightly out of fashion polo shirt, probably vintage Men's Express. He threw back a chug from his longneck Bud Light and continued to holler.

Torrents of the F-bomb rained down on my fellow Chili's diners, who also turned to gawk at the man whose Baby Back Ribs were apparently not grilled to mouthwatering perfection.

Yea, that's right, you food snobs. We were at Chili's. Not my favorite dining establishment, but our Christmas vacation in West Texas only offered so many ops for gourmet eating. My husband and I were thrilled just to be out on a date with free babysitting courtesy of my folks. We could have been under the golden arches and still have been pleased as punch.

So when that man started yelling at his just-out-of-diapers waiter, I couldn't help but stare. It was Chili's after all. CHILI'S! Not that I think that eating in a fancier place justifies being mean to your server, but I was shocked that anyone could have such high expectations for a restaurant decorated with 1970s framed photos of chili cook-offs. And I was shocked that anyone would resort to loud public cursing over something as trivial as a dinner for four with drinks and appetizers that'll cost less than $50.

As I understand it, Chili's food is actually created in some magical Chili's factory, flash frozen, and then shipped to the restaurants where it is re-cooked on site. That's why all the food tastes the same. So unless this jerk's Guiltless Chicken Sandwich accidentally came out of the kitchen with a side of guilt or it was still clucking, I can't imagine that there was anything gone awry enough to warrant a full-body Olympic cuss-out.

I kept staring. His wife/girlfriend/partner, a hunched over, portly woman with a limp ponytail, sat dejected in the booth. I wondered if she (a) was embarrassed by his horrific behavior, (b) felt sadly used to it, or (c) also liked to scream at service people when the mood struck.

"Quit staring!" my husband Jeff stage-whispered to me from across our bar table. "People carry guns around here and he's already in a shootin' mood!"

But I couldn't help myself. My gaze traveled to another table next to the offending adult group. Two elementary school-aged children, who obviously belonged to the unrefined man, picked listlessly at their chicken tenders. Nice, I thought. Way to model decent adulthood in front of the kids. And some say that etiquette is dead.

What could the youngsters be thinking about their dad's upchuck of obscenities? Maybe "Gee willikers! When I get big I'm gonna learn to swear like a real man! Isn't my daddy awesome! He learns me new stuff every dolgone day!"

The thoughtful, intelligent-eyed girl probably bemoaned the nasty, brutish short temper of her father and quietly planned her future rebellion involving a shaved head and several strategically placed cranial tattoos.

The food server, a pimply-faced college student, handled his sorry excuse for a customer with grace and panache. He outclassed the inebriated hillbilly by roughly four Emily Post books and ten weeks of Miss Manners columns.

"No problem, sir," was all the wise young man uttered as he nodded his head and whisked away the unsatisfactory corporate dining experience.

I wanted to cry and hug this young waiter. If he had been our server I would have tipped him beyond his wildest dreams. His name might have appeared in my final will and testament. I silently issued a prayerful apology on behalf of the human race for the unbridled ugliness that probably ruined the poor kid's shift.

And while I feared for the future of human kindness, I also pondered why that jackass customer hated his own life so much that he had to humiliate the Chili's server to feel important.

I hope it helped. I hope he felt so dadgum great about himself that his self-esteem soared through the roof and he went home and started a non-profit foundation dedicated to helping others out of their own mire of unrealized dreams and heartaches.

I hope that someone much more brave (or drunk) than I was had the nerve to ask the Potty Mouth if he kisses his mama with those dirty lips.

I hope that someone washed his mouth out with soap.

I also hope that the waiter hocked a nice loogie in Mr. Tacky's Bloomin' Onion.

Later on I asked my brother-in-law, a professional waiter, if people really do mean things to the food of rude patrons.

"Oh, you don't even want to know," he replied. I made a quick mental tally of all the times I may have (deservedly) eaten human phlegm as a result of my own uncivilized restaurant behavior. I also made a quick note to self to be as kind as a kindergarten teacher on a yoga high on future dining out excursions.

The Post-Christmas Blues

The winter holidays are already fading into digital photoshopped memories, but sometimes I spot snatches of Christmas leftovers: A forgotten wreath swinging askew on a side door. Half-hung Christmas lights dangling limply from the window of the apartment building across the street. An abandoned tinsel town in the window of an appliance repair shop.

All of these observations, including a drooping tree left to brown at the curb on January 25, can evoke a bit of the post-holiday melancholy. It reminds me that the fun, food, and family hoopla of the yuletide season are officially packed away until next year.

Since most of the people who share my husband's and my DNA live halfway across the continent, it is especially poignant to say good bye to the time of year when we know we can all get together and delight in annoying the crap out of each other.

It's hard to let go of Christmas and enter back into the real world.

This year, however, I have had assistance with combating the inevitable culture shock of leaving Santaland and beginning a bumpy re-entry into the post-new year's football onslaught. This year, I have learned that my always brilliant two-year-old (almost three by her estimates) possesses an uncanny ability to compose a song befitting to appropriate occasions.

Shortly after we returned from my family's holiday vacation to Texas, Grace, my daughter, learned that the Big Event was officially done. No more presents. No more stockings. No more gingerbread houses.

"Christmas is done?" she asked. "But I want more!" I couldn't agree *more*.

Upon reflection of the benediction of her new favorite day, Grace composed the following ditty. Now, imagine a small child, with a most earnest voice and furrowed brow, singing this song in a slow, high-pitched falsetto as she goes about her daily business of tasting Play-doh and decorating the kitchen floor with stickers:

Sleighbells are falling.
Santa is walking.
In the rain.
Looking for his elves.

Now, as somebody more important than me once said, writing about music is like dancing about architecture.

But allow yourself to close your eyes for a minute a take in the melancholy of those simple existential lyrics. And you may agree with me that I think we have a future blueswoman on our hands here. With her fiery red hair, Grace may very well be the next Bonnie Raitt!

As gloomy as it may be, this sweet song has lifted our household out of its post-Christmas wallowing. We all join together and sing the chorus several times a day as we celebrate, rather than mourn, the annual transition of post-holiday letdown. Instead of bemoaning the loss of a beautiful time of year, our family now honors the cyclical nature of life by loudly lifting our voices for the Post-Christmas Blues.

It is cathartic. It is healing. And it is funny.

However, as we look ahead to other important days in the lives of kids, most notably the upcoming third birthday of our budding composer, I see the tenure of the holiday song nearing its inevitable end. Just like the holidays must be fleeting and brief, so that they may be special, so must our song be held in reserve.

Just this morning, I tried to get a hearty round of "Sleighbells Are Falling" going as I hustled Grace out the door for her childcare co-op. But she stopped me mid-verse.

"I don't sing that song anymore, Mama." She looked up at me with all of the seriousness and openness that can only emanate from the face of a small child.

"Because Christmas is over," she said.

Yes, but we know it will come back next year. Along with a soulful rendition of the Post-Christmas Blues.

Radio Free West Texas

When I was in 8th grade, living in Midland, Texas, I used to religiously listen
to a nightly radio program called Radio Free West Texas. Students at nearby
Odessa Community College put on the show, an obvious homage to REM's
alt-nerd anthem, "Radio Free Europe," and they spent the hours from 10 to
midnight spinning requests from the call-ins of West Texas' best collection
of outcasts.

Being only thirteen, and appropriately sheltered by my parents, I was
supposed to be in bed by 10, supposed to be done with my homework, off
the phone and getting some rest for school the next day. Being thirteen,
I ignored my parents' rules and sat up until midnight most nights, my ear
pressed to my small plastic boombox, excitedly breathing in every subversive
melody. I loved the illicit sense of voyeurism that I felt when I heard the
dedications played on air, especially when I recognized the names of the
various cool older kids who knew much more about underground music
than I did.

"This Dead Milkmen song goes out to Erin from Anne. Your Camaro
is truly bitchin', she says." Then a scuffed up record would blast a heretofore
unknown skate-rock song from my cheap Sony.

I heard contemporary new wave and punk rock bands like Smiths, the
Cure, Siouxsie and the Banshees, the Dead Kennedys, Depeche Mode and
Minor Threat. Then sometimes the eighteen-year-old DJ gave us an old school
education with the Sex Pistols, the Ramones, and the Velvet Underground.
I learned all about how to be cool from these late night sessions. I learned
which band names I needed to drop to impress the cute skater boys I so
admired. I learned which cassettes to pounce on in the bins at Musicland or
Record Bar at the Midland Park Mall. I learned about the secret lives of the

glamorous older kids I idolized from our common community theatre youth troupe experiences.

We were the classic geeks, misfits and weirdos that populate the fringes of any small American town. We were the kids with Mohawks, the vegetarians, the honors students with ambitions to escape to NYU, the artists, the kids who read Nietzsche and Proust with a sincere desire to get it. We were the skaters, the poets, the Goths, the Mods, the gay kids, the Dungeons and Dragons nerds, and the Theatre People. In a larger-sized city, we would have all been separated into our own distinct cliques. But in the pint-sized society of Midland, Texas we had to stick together for solidarity or else get our asses individually beat. Even the girls sometimes. My best friend, Susan, had her life regularly threatened in P.E. class for being too "diff'ernt."

The stress of having to daily outmaneuver the intentional kicks and trips of the bullying hair metal girls caused Susan to stop menstruating for six months. The doctor said it was a biological reaction that many women have to war and famine: don't make a baby if you won't live to raise it.

As one of the poetry-writing, black-clad theatre geeks, I latched onto the music of Radio Free West Texas with all of the passion of any self-absorbed teenager. This was my music. Its lyrics spoke to me, as if each musician had read my angst-ridden young mind, as if he or she understood my struggle to find a place where I fit in. The first time I heard Morrissey sing that he wore black on the outside because black is how he felt on the inside I cried with relief and empathy, shuddering to imagine how anyone could so accurately nail my unique brand of pain. Finally, I found some lyrics that got it right. These were words that superseded my hometown, where I regularly saw George W. Bush at church and we achieved international fame for a baby falling down a well. No more Huey Lewis or Morris Day and the Time for me. I was a full-on convert to Alternative music.

Back then, around the mid-80s, what we called "Alternative" music was still actually an alternative to the mainstream. The music I heard on Radio Free West Texas never came up on the playlists of the top 40, classic rock, or country music stations that populated the spinning dial of my radio alarm clock. By listening to obscure tunes that most kids in my hometown never heard of, I slightly redeemed my adolescent inferiority complex, at least in the music department. Knowledge of unusual bands gave me status, access, and respect among the unified weirdo subculture. One of the proudest moments of my fourteen-year-old life came when a cool skater guy who sat next to me in social studies class loudly acknowledged to his friends, "Robin's cool. She likes the Dead Kennedys." The boys flopped their asymmetrical bangs in approval and I felt more regal than the Homecoming Queen.

The life of a junior high girl is never easy. Well, maybe for a certain select crew of beautiful blond girls it seems easy, but I doubt that even those kids just coast by. It is a tumultuous, hormonal time, full of changing bodies and a craving for approval. After trying and failing miserably to fit into the giggling cheerleading cliché, I found a beautiful solace in the freak-embracing arms of music. My music. Alternative music. Music only to be found between the hours of ten and midnight, way down at the far left of the dial on Radio Free West Texas.

A Socially Irresponsible Stroll Through My Neighborhood

By the time you finish reading this essay, you will think I am a depraved, cold-hearted, unfeeling subhuman. Someone on the level of Monty Burns, J.R. Ewing or Dick Cheney. In other words, some of the things I am about to reveal will possibly offend you.

But I want to be honest. When I take a walk in my San Francisco neighborhood, sometimes I like to sidestep certain annoying people or things. And I do have a certain guilty pleasure in artfully avoiding that which is detrimental to me having a decent walk.

You see, my family has one car. So we daily negotiate which adult will drive the Honda, depending on the whims of scheduling and public transportation. On the days when my husband takes the car, my daughter and I tend to get creative. Sometimes we take the train to various parks or child-friendly destinations, or mooch rides from friends. But most days we run errands on foot with my kiddo cruising in her stroller or on her tricycle.

Our jaunts up to the main commercial corridor of my neighborhood usually take an hour or more, roundtrip. These walks offer opportunities for fitness, fresh air, and a sense of community.

But there are also weird people. And sometimes I am simply not in a state of mind to deal with a weird person every ten feet. Especially when my kid is wailing, my feet are tired, my throat is parched and I just want to buy my dang stamps and toilet paper and get home. So when these days occur, I eschew all moral responsibility as a good member of this society and I take a circuitous route that allows me to avoid interacting with all manner of bothersome folks.

When we leave the house for our walk, we first head up a street that is loaded with pedestrians, cars, and trains. On days when I don't want to haggle with confrontation, I am careful to stay on the west side of this street to avoid the Dog People hanging out around the pet store.

Offensive item number one: Sometimes I am very annoyed at the Dog People.

In a city where "I have a dog and I vote" bumper stickers outnumber "Baby on Board" window tags by ten to one, such a statement could indeed cause rabid throngs of "Dog is my co-pilot" citizens to toss me into the Bay faster than you can throw a tennis ball at a Yorkshire Terrier.

So let me just say that I really do love dogs. I grew up in a house full of dogs. I love the well-cared-for dogs of my friends, my family, and my neighbors. I know from experience that they are wonderful, precious companions. It's just that, since I have lived in San Francisco, some of the dog owners have created a bad name for the Dog People.

It's not just the feces in front of my house every morning or the clean fresh smell of urine on my stoop. It's the giant unleashed Rottweilers that run up and thrust their snouts into my two-year-old's face. The doggy owners usually laugh and go, "Isn't that cute? Killer just lo-oves babies!" Meanwhile, my kid furiously lashes her arms and head about in terror.

After successfully maneuvering around the piles of fresh dog poo and avoiding free-roaming slobbering Pit Bulls, we arrive at the main drag ready to run our errands. The first group to steer clear of on this street is the cluster of homeless people who lurk around the parking lot of the grocery store.

Offensive item number two: Sometimes I go out of my way to evade sketchy panhandlers.

It is impossible to avoid homeless people in San Francisco. It is a tragic, heart-wrenching problem, argued by many as the biggest political issue in this City. Should we give them cash? Better social programs? I don't know. I am not an expert in public policy nor am I planning to run for mayor. I do know that some of the regulars in our neighborhood are friendly and superficially harmless—like the guy in front of the taqueria with whom we regularly exchange pleasantries. But there are others who seem far less stable. It's just a mother's gut instinct.

Once we pass the grocery store on the opposite side of its parking lot, we must quickly cross the street, sometimes jaywalking, so that we can avoid going past the Starbucks at peak hours. This is the time that all of the solicitors for various non-profits hang out and harass passers-by.

Offensive item number three: I loathe being put on the spot by street fund-raisers, no matter how good the cause.

During times of busy foot-traffic, college kids are paid minimum wage to jump in the path of pedestrians. They yell, "Excuse me! Do you care about defeating the Republicans in the next election?" Or "Do you have a minute for the future of California's environment?" If you say no you are a jerk. If you say yes you have to sit down with them on a bench for thirty minutes of spiel while your child goes berserk. As a former fundraiser, I want to yell, "Get to the pitch already!"

Once I sneak by the college-kid solicitors, I can stay on the north side of the street for quite a while. This ensures I circumvent the political petition people who park in front of the post office or, on Saturdays, outside of the Farmers' Market.

Offensive item number four: I don't like filling out a thousand petitions on the street to support political actions that remind me of my total ignorance on the Governator's latest crusade to end the free intake of oxygen in the state of California.

"Excuse me, ma'am. Are you registered to vote in California?"

The first time I heard this I thought it was a voting drive and I immediately piped up that of course I am. "Good, then can you please sign these twelve petitions to introduce propositions numbers 68 through 79 on the November ballot? We'll need your full address, phone number, email, date of birth and signature on each form. Thank you!"

They neglect to say, "While you are distracted with scribbling down your college thesis in triplicate, we'll repay the favor by allowing your toddler to climb off her tricycle and run into the street."

So now I sometimes take the long way when I see the petition people lined up with their clipboards.

All of this avoidance is refreshing. My walk goes well, my kid is happy, and I don't have to keep saying "NO" to every person I pass by.

However, there is a small caveat that I must contend with when trying to weasel out of directly saying "NO" to so many people. I must walk past the storefront window of a kooky old person who insists on displaying, for the entire world to view, every racist, xenophobic, homophobic, hate-spewing idea that most people move to San Francisco to escape.

One of my favorites, a direct "screw you" to the City's strong multi-ethic populations, is a simple hand-lettered sign taped in the window that shouts, "ENGLISH spoken here!!!"

It is a creepy display, sometimes nasty and often entertaining, but it is not something that I want to explain to my child just yet. As soon as she learns to read I am going to have to explain concepts like "foreigners go home" and "looney liberals" to her.

However, as bizarre as this window may be, and as little as I like to patronize its 1950s rhetoric with my eyeballs, some days I prefer to stroll past it rather than fend off the advances of yet another person on the street who wants something.

This fascinating window also tends to push me back into the arms of humanity. After an afternoon of avoiding people and situations that aren't my cup of tea, I am always struck by the militant storefront messenger. He must be so terrified of encountering anyone even slightly different from himself that he can only respond by posting angry tirades in the front of his shop. Do I want to end up like him?

At the end of my socially irresponsible stroll, I finally get home. My weary feet throb from pounding miles of concrete in ill-fitting shoes. Grace demands that I carry her (and the diaper bag and the bag of groceries and her toy baby) up the flight of stairs to our front door.

As I crash into the living room, I realize that, instead of feeling guilty for saying no, no, no to every person who crosses my path, I feel guilty for hiding from these people in the first place.

But my refusal to deal with confrontation does shorten my walk by a good forty-five minutes. My child has not had a public meltdown in front of the flower shop and I artfully dodged being scared by German Shepherds of unknown obedience school pedigree.

Some days it's better to just choose the guilty pleasure and risk feeling like Monty Burns.

First Day of Preschool

We walk into the carefully organized classroom and the panic sets in. Not in Grace. In me. I notice every grubby detail that I must have missed at the orientation last month. Those kitchen toys are just jumbled in a pile. And when were those costumes last washed? The room is too quiet. Those cool toys are up too high where the kids can't reach them. The playground looks wet and cold. There are only boys here. Where are the girls? Will Grace be the only girl?

I am wild-eyed, surveying the room like a lioness ready to devour any threat to her young. Grace hugs my leg, prompting me to get it together.

"Let's put your things in your cubby, ok?" I say to my daughter. This suggestion is exciting and she detaches herself from my leg to unload her backpack. We take a casual tour of the room, where the toys don't look so bad. In fact, some of the work centers seem pretty cool. I make a note to copy an idea for Play-doh accessories back home.

We go outside and Grace helps her teacher, Christina, to get the sand toys out of the storage shed. I see a daddy, who is wearing a baby in a sling, dropping off his little boy. I breathe a sigh of relief that there are some other cool parents. Then I silently scold myself for thinking that using a sling makes someone cool. A youngish mom with unusual facial piercings brings her daughter by and I am relieved to see a girl. Again I scold myself for my bizarre attachment to gender balance. She's not even three! Who cares if she plays with boys or girls?

After spending a few minutes watching Grace dig in the sand, Jeff and I announce that it is time for us to leave. I crouch down at kid level and Grace clings to me harder than I have ever felt. Her arms envelope my neck and she crawls up my body like she is trying to go back inside my womb.

"Please take me home with you! Please don't go!" she begs.

"Why don't you walk us to the door?" I suggest.

She does and the teacher's aide silently follows behind. At the door Grace cries and begs again. I fight back my own tears. "I love you so much, Grace. And I am so proud of you. You are going to have a great time today, and I will come back to get you later. I promise."

She still won't let go. I start to stand up, to force the separation, no matter how painful. Grace grabs the scarf from my neck so that it unwinds as I stand. "Can I keep this until you get back?" she says.

"Of course you can."

And just like that she switches into chatty, happy Grace mode. She turns to Roxie, the teacher's aide, and says "This is my mommy's scarf and I am going to keep it for her until she comes back." Then she turns and heads out to play.

And I feel ok. We leave the classroom and peek through the one-way observation window in the hall. The scarf is knotted around Grace's neck and she is chatting away with Roxie.

I remember the game we played yesterday, initiated by Grace, where she said that she was the mommy taking me to school. She asked me to cry when she left and then she said she would give me something to hold until she got back. I can't believe I didn't proactively remember that game this morning. Kids are so amazing at making sure their needs are met, and yesterday she was definitely letting me know what would give her comfort. Grace knew what would make her feel better and, when I forgot to give her a little something of mine, she went ahead and took my scarf. Simply amazing.

When I pick Grace up she doesn't want to leave. "But I'm still playing, Mama!"

I finally persuade her to head out to the car with a promise of a box of soymilk that waits for her. In the hallway she talks and talks about her day. The words are a blurry chatter of kidspeak and I have trouble making it all out. But something does jump out at me.

"I had fun, fun, fun at school today. It is full of love."

I am so relieved and grateful to hear this that I almost burst into tears. My heart is also incredibly full of love.

Grand Mess Auto

I really, really want to buy an additional car for our family of three.

Some of you loyal readers may be fortunate enough to not understand what I am talking about.

"Do you mean that you need a third car? Something 'just for fun' like an off-road camping van or a sporty little Beemer to take to Napa for the weekend?" you might ask.

No. Although the thought of cruising through the Wine Country (childless) in a sleek convertible makes me want to cash in my retirement fund and run to the nearest luxury import dealer.

We need a second car.

Let me back up and explain. We live in San Francisco, where the cost of car insurance and gas alone is equivalent to a down payment on a nice little condo in Tucson. Add parking issues and the ease of public transportation to the mix and you end up with many families (like us) who only have one car. For many, this has nothing to do with the ability to actually buy a second vehicle. Some of my most fancy-panted, well-to-do friends are members of one-car families.

Single car living has its benefits. Besides the money-saving perks, we feel good about using fewer resources and putting less toxic exhaust into our ever-warming atmosphere. We enjoy the health benefits of running around town on foot instead of by auto. And we also thrive on the vibrant sense of community that exists when we take on the City without a big metal box between us and everyone else.

BUT, (And you knew there would be a big but, didn't you?) life with only one car can also really stink. Especially for a woman who spent most of her life in Texas, where going without a car is not even an option.

A couple of recent transportation fiascos recently drove this point home. No pun intended.

The first disaster took place at my daughter's childcare co-operative on a day when Daddy took the car to work. I walked Grace to the co-op playground in her jogging stroller, a normal activity in our world, and dropped her off for the morning.

After I walked back home, a sudden downpour left my friends at the park in a messy situation. The on-duty mama was forced to negotiate three kids, two carseats, one car and an immediate need for evacuation. I was back at home with no car and no extra carseat, since Grace's carseat was safe and dry in the parking garage of Daddy's work.

Sheer embarrassment and a fear of ramifications from Child Protective Services prevent me from revealing how we solved the dilemma.

If that weren't enough, a mere three days later we had another car trauma.

I planned for the trip to the Exploratorium museum all weekend. The journey was too far for us to take the necessary train and two buses, and Jeff needed to drive to an offsite meeting. So I bargained with a generous mama friend to mooch a ride to our playdate at the awesome museum way over in the Marina neighborhood.

The morning of the big day arrived, and Jeff drove off to work with the carseat still in the back of the car. By the time my buddy arrived and the faux pas came to light, the best I could do was to call Jeff in his meeting to holler at him.

Grace stood in the driveway wailing while I tried my best to explain that we couldn't go to the museum because we didn't have a seat for her in the car. I ended up bribing her with ice cream, a new pair of scissors and a train ride to her best little girlfriend's house.

So now I always get the car on co-op days and I'm much more careful to make sure we take out the carseat before Jeff takes the Honda to work. But those incidents, especially the rainy day chaos, left me unnerved. What if we got stranded somewhere? What if we had an emergency?

I started in on my whiney campaign for a second car. Jeff agreed that it would be a nice asset and that we'll get right on that as soon as our backyard money tree starts blossoming this spring.

Meanwhile, my mom made an excellent suggestion. "I don't think you need a second car," she said. "You just need a second carseat."

Good point. But I'm still vying for a kid-friendly BMW convertible. And a weekend in Napa.

Preschool Update

So here we are, chugging along in a full-fledged preschool routine, with my daughter spending two whole, long days in the dirty sand and finger paint-filled world of the three-year-old. I can't say that I've fully become accustomed to it, but I no longer cry each time I say good-bye.

Since Grace has started spending two days a week in the care of highly-trained professionals, I've rediscovered the age-old principal that work expands or contracts to fill the amount of time available. I suddenly don't know how I ever got anything done before Grace went to preschool.

I have piles and lists and sticky notes and email documents of chores and tasks that stretch beyond my capabilities. And even though I spend two solid days a week puttering around the house while my kid is at school, I never get it all done.

Part of my inability to complete a simple round of dusting or filing may relate to the fact that I now try to offer my undivided attention to Grace when she is around. I used to multitask in her presence, flailing away at scrubbing the toilet or catching up on emails while Grace played nearby. Now I save all these to-do items for the long stretches of time when we are apart.

Here's another thing I am getting used to:

San Francisco has become a whole new city these days. Since we moved here when I was pregnant, my entire urban experience has always been modified by the presence of a small person either in my belly or in tow. When Grace is at school, I now take the MUNI buses and trains with ease, all alone and unburdened by a bulging belly, strollers, slings, diaper bags, toy babies, lunchboxes, or extra undies that have been part of my ensemble for so long.

Yet I feel oddly vulnerable without Grace by my side in the City. I am so used to traipsing about town while managing her needs, that I am suddenly naked when spending so much time alone in the great wide open. Not that her presence protects me from any real threat, but with her by my side I always have a purpose. That purpose may merely be a walk to the end of the block to look at the trains, but it is still a reason to be out of the house and in the world.

When I leave the house with Grace by my side I always have a reason to avoid interacting with people I deem annoying, without seeming like I'm totally rude for not signing that Greenpeace petition. Now I have to come up with a better excuse other than my kid needs to get to a potty. When Grace isn't with me, I also lose my chance to talk to strangers without looking like a maniac, striking up conversations with other mamas and daddies who are out and about.

Since Grace has become a preschooler, I find myself nostalgic for those lazy unscheduled days, just a year ago, when a mama buddy and I would call each other after naptime to decide if we should go jogging our just slob out in one of our backyards.

Now my friend is back to work, full-time, and her kiddo is in preschool all day. In order to plan a successful playdate, we must align school schedules, nap times, bed times and the seventh house of Aquarius.

But here is the upside.

Grace loves, loves, loves going to school. She stays later and later each school day because she cries when Jeff or I show up to drag her home. She has a messy, silly, giggly bunch of new friends. She has gentle, dynamic, thoughtful teachers who inspire her to push her mind and body to exciting new limits.

And I love, love, love my time to write, to earn a little extra income through my piddly contract jobs, to do some yoga, to take a long walk over the San Francisco hills, and to feel like the archetypical housewife as I catch up on laundry while parked on my butt in front of *Oprah*.

So even though this transition is most bittersweet, I know it is the right one for our family. And by getting her started in preschool a little early, I am avoiding the college-admissions-like crush that is the San Francisco preschool process. (But that is a whole 'nother story...)

Besides, if I ever want to remember why I love these feelings of freedom, all I need to do is wait for summer vacation.

MySpace or Yours?

Sometimes when I procrastinate writing this column or pretend like I'm cool, I channel surf for "Fuse," which is like MTV except that it actually plays music videos. After glazing over in front of a Korn or Ghostface Killah song, meant for an audience half my age, I usually proceed to freak out as I consider the adolescent world my daughter will inherit.

Not only are the videos usually beyond the pale in terms of misogynistic sex imagery and glorious gratuitous violence, but they are surrounded by a seizure-inducing stream of "live chat" emailed and text-messaged in by their teenage audience.

"Yo. Peace to my crunk peeps. Luv4eva."

"Droppin N2 holla."

"Kickit wit ur cuz. B cool."

Huh?

I'm not a virtuous, Christian-pop-only prude. Nor am I total geek. Well, maybe not. I tend to cling precariously to the outermost edge of the monolith of indie rock via the downloads of my music-obsessed better half. And I actually like certain newfangled bands like the Killers and Interpol, bands that sound like recycled new wave from my high school years.

But I sometimes feel like a member of Tom Brokaw's Greatest Generation when trying to stay on top of youth culture in anticipation of my daughter's future. I just can't keep up. By the time I get my blog going, blogs will be as nerdy and unhip as I am. By the time I master text messaging the kids will be sending psychic shout-outs via their "Intel Inside" brain implants.

My husband says that we should get accounts on MySpace.com now, well before Grace gets old enough to sign up for her little piece of internet heaven. (According to the tween marketing experts she will be ready in about two years at the tender age of five.) This way we can reserve a really cool login name for her before they are all taken. At this stage of her development, all I can think that we should secure for her is something along the lines of eatzsand, luv2screem, or napsis4babeez.

I think MySpace might be fun, but I have no idea what sort of nerdy mumbo jumbo I would post on this website, which describes itself as "a place for friends." My friends are all too busy chasing their children around and earning a living to spend their time instant messaging, updating their blogs and posting new pictures. MySpace is for young, childless people with lots and lots and lots of free time.

I'm just glad we didn't have MySpace when I was locked in the sweaty hormonal embrace of adolescence. The thought of a permanent, easily accessible homage to my teen angst makes me want to curl my crusty toes into balls of cringing mortification and hide inside my box of old Cure posters and Jello Biafra tapes. I can just imagine the content.

Upon entering my personal page you would be greeted by a photo of a sullen-faced, pimply girl with very tall bangs wearing a black t-shirt that says "Depeche Mode, Music for the Masses Tour, 1987." If you clicked on "MY PICTURES" you would see a shot of the back of my head, featuring a trendy halo of shaved skull, only revealed when the rest of the hair is up in a ponytail. So very cool and nonconformist. Har har.

These would be my MySpace INTERESTS:

GENERAL. Hi, I'm a sixteen year old high school student in Midland, Texas. I like drama, reading profound books, writing poetry, wearing black clothes, dating boys who make my parents nervous, and slinking around feeling sorry for myself. I dislike jocks, muscle cars, and snooty girls who pretend to be stupid to make muscle car jocks like them.

MUSIC. Anything new wave or alternative!!! Morrissey. The Smiths. The Cure. Love and Rockets. Bauhaus. Ministry. Front 242. Sisters of Mercy. New Order. Dead Kennedys. No country! No metal! (except skate rock). No preppy Top 40!

(If you have noted how my general disposition is framed mostly in the negative, you may be on to something.)

MOVIES. *Pretty in Pink* (because I am in love with Duckie), *The Lost Boys* (because I am in love with sexy Goth vampire boys), *Koyaanisquati* (because I'm really deep and intellectual)

Blogs would include an ongoing debate with my best friend over certain prescient topics. (1.) Can you be the truest, most dedicated fan of Morrissey and not be a vegetarian? (2.) If you only like music by the Clash post-1982, does that make you a poseur? (3.) Is Laura really a narc?

Can you imagine the humiliation of having such drivel still lurking around the web? It's bad enough to have it tucked away in my high school journals.

I found out about all these scintillating categories of self-expression while snooping around MySpace.com after Jeff made his wise suggestion. But I couldn't stay on the website for too long. Not only was it boring in that vapid, teenage sort of been-there-before-and don't-wanna-go-back sort of way, some of it was downright alarming.

And then I saw a video that gave me even bigger heebie jeebies.

Warning to parents of small children: if you really want to get scared about the upcoming teenage years, just watch this clip I saw on fastandloud. com. It features actual photos that have been taken off of MySpace and set to the tune of Whitney Houston's classic *The Greatest Love of All*. A skin-curdling montage of drunken, toked-up, gun-toting, half-naked teenagers creepily crawls past, making me want to lock my kid up in a nunnery for the next few decades.

I know I sound like an old fart, like every generation of moms and dads since Elvis got all pelvis-y back on Ed Sullivan. I sound like a total hypocrite who has forgotten her own weirdo teenage rebellion. And maybe that's true. But Elvis didn't go online trolling for an underage girl to molest. He did it the old fashioned way, by getting permission from the girl's parents to marry her.

And just in case there is a possibility of remaining a mindful parent amidst the maddening rush of teenage techie-marketing and adolescent internet product pimping, I am going to try to keep up.

Even if it means harking back to my John Hughes movie-fueled, black-clad, teenage drama queen days so that I can try to relate to my daughter. Even if it means starting my own geek-mama blog on MySpace.

Flying the Coop

Around eighteen-months ago, a friend called me up with a serendipitous solution to my craving for affordable childcare.

"How 'bout we start a co-op?" she said.

"Huh? A co-operative?"

The word co-op brought up images from my days in Austin: a communal dorm where drugs oozed from the walls and where my sexually confused best friend from high school ended up living; an intimidating natural foods grocery store where I always felt too bourgeois and geeky to ask which aisle contained the Velveeta; a University of Texas bookstore that overflowed burnt orange Longhorn paraphernalia.

"Yea, a co-op," said my mommy-pal. "For babysitting. We can have a couple of parents watch four or five kids at a time and the others get the morning off."

Oh. My. God. What a fantastic idea.

"I'm in!" I practically screamed into the phone.

And that's how the Hummingbirds began.

We initially gathered four families and struggled through hectic, unstructured playgroups at one-another's homes. Two parents tried valiantly to entertain four toddlers for three hours while the other two went off, carefree and childfree into the foggy city.

No one knew quite how to organize these ad hoc playgroups, and the kids sometimes went a little berserk. By the end of the morning the on-duty mothers were usually filthy, stinking and exhausted. But then our group grew, and an angelic preschool teacher-turned stay-at-home-mama joined the fold.

This patron saint of toddlers quickly suggested that we start meeting in public parks as often as possible. This way no one's house would get destroyed by a herd of yogurt-smearing children. The host kid wouldn't freak out at sharing his or her toys. And all the little dudes could run amuck and get their climb on without upending the dining room table.

So we started spending two mornings a week at a hilltop playground, and over the course of a year, we saw our children grow from toddlers into bona fide little kids.

Nowadays they hike and climb hills. They monkey all over the monkey bars. They cruise on the Big Kid Swings instead of the mommy-back-breaking Baby Swings. They wash hands before snack, and eat together at a community picnic table. They go potty and they dress themselves.

They try very hard not to hit and push and kick and bite each other. They share. Sometimes.

In short, they have grown up a little.

And always, on our hikes along the steep trails that line the hilly park, we sing. A favorite song is a little made-up ditty about looking for a Hummingbird out a window, accompanied by a choreographed arm-flapping. Whenever it is time to get the attention of five scattered two- and three-year-olds, the Hummingbird song never fails to do the trick.

Like zombies hearing the dinner bell clang for brains, the kids automatically drop their sand shovels or piles of rocks and stare out into space as soon as they hear the initial "Hummingbird, hummingbird, at my window…"

One by one, they look around, searching for the origin of their call to gather. Then, like Pavlovian mongrels, they wander in a daze toward the singer until all five are huddled in a clump, each kid flapping his or her hands, Hummingbird-style.

I often spend my turns as the on-duty mama simply marveling at the uncanny social development going on at the Hummingbird playgroup. In my clearly biased opinion our kids are experiencing something magical, a mystical, once-in-a-cosmic-lifetime convergence of families and schedules and personalities and lifestyles. Of course we have a few glitches every once in a while, but I am not exaggerating when I say that we usually have a blissful situation for everyone.

The kids feel safe and comfortable, being cared for by moms, and sometimes dads, who are the closest thing to family we all have in San Francisco. All of the members of our group are from somewhere else, so we truly need each other for childcare and mental health support. The mamas love having guaranteed, pre-arranged time to work or run errands without worrying about the quality of care for our children. And the children love having guaranteed playdates with a gang that has become the best of friends.

Besides the decision to breastfeed, starting our co-op is the one parenting choice I made with absolutely no doubts, no misgivings and no regrets. I would do it all over again.

Perhaps because of our wild success with the co-op, the transition to preschool initially made me as much or more nervous than Grace, for we suddenly left the tightly controlled social networks of my own design and entered the random chaos of a classroom. Thank God we decided to have some overlap, with Grace attending both preschool and co-op for the first semester.

Because at co-op I am in control. The playgroup consists of families who are all on the same page, or at least reading the same book, on issues like television, junk food, corporal punishment, and even politics. It is homogenous. It is predictable. I know that no one will teach Grace about semi-automatics or the F-word when she is at co-op.

Preschool, on the other hand, marks our family's entry into great social experiment of group education. It is a recipe with an unpredictable outcome. Will she meet kids from abusive homes who are already becoming little bullies themselves? Or what about kids who already watch *CSI* or even *SpongeBob Squarepants*? Will she come home begging for Fruity Pebbles or toxic blue yogurt because some cool four-year-old has it in his lunchbox?

Preschool is one of those great childhood rites of passage where I suddenly have no say over who my kid hangs out with. Fortunately all the children in Grace's school have parents who go to school or work at the university where Jeff teaches, so we at least have that in common.

Still, I dread the day when we will have to cut the lifeline of co-op, to sever the tether that connects us to our chosen family when family is so far away. Grace knows most of these mamas better than her own aunt, although it breaks my heart to admit. The dissolution of our group with the advent of preschool for all the kids, although inevitable, is terrifying.

Like with many of Grace's childhood milestones, I both celebrate and grieve her upcoming graduation from co-op, knowing that once we leave this beautiful, transitory, fleeting moment we will never ever go back.

Dispatches From the Texas Hill Country

In case you were wondering, I love visiting Texas!

I especially love how some of the things that used to bug the tarnation out of me when I lived here are now more charming and endearing than a sack full of Southern Belles.

I now love the way that Texans tend to lose their ever-lovin' minds over sports, and the way that college football is more important than religion to many native Texans. I have also recently learned to appreciate how a good long "y'all" sounds in person (much better than over the phone.)

Other things I love and miss about Texas:

Water-skiing Lake LBJ on a Tuesday morning when the surface of the lake is still as smooth as glass and everyone else is at work.

Having enough old friends that I never lack for company at the lake. Even on a Tuesday morning.

Austin's South Congress Avenue, where I can spend my cash on everything from cowboy boots to sushi to live music, and where the (keepin' it weird) Austin Motel boasts a sign reading "So Close Yet So Far Out!"

Cute tattooed waitresses at the Magnolia Café who call me Honey.

Sitting on the porch after the kids go to sleep, drinking beer, and watching the fireflies.

Views of the Texas sunset over the Hill Country while driving along twisted highways with names like "Devil's Backbone."

Getting the "Texas Friendly" wave from the driver in the pickup that passes me along that same hilly highway.

Food, food, FOOD!!! Namely, Salt Lick BBQ, Tex-Mex enchiladas, chili con queso, migas, breakfast tacos, Amy's ice cream and Texas microbrewed beer.

Not having to explain how my uncle and my father have accidentally shot off a finger and a toe, respectively. (Texans just get this sort of thing.)

The way my husband starts calling other men "sir" when we are here, especially the police who just might take you in if you don't.

The way my daughter picks up on it and starts to demonstrate a modicum of Southern manners at least ten percent of the time.

Good friends and old family. Wait, I mean old friends and good family.

Things I don't love or miss about Texas:

(Note to Lone Star Loved Ones: Put away your shotguns. This part of the list really just serves to make me feel better once I head back out of here to NorCal and long for a plate of Chuy's enchiladas or a dip in Barton Springs.)

The Texas State Legislature and all of their many inanities. My personal favorite was a refusal to name a stretch of Texas highway after Texas legend Willie Nelson because he was deemed to be a liberal and therefore allied with Osama Bin Laden, Saddam Hussein and probably Satan himself.

Having to drive EVERYWHERE. And if you decide to walk, the heat not only beats you down, but everyone stares at you from behind the tinted windows of their SUV like you are some kind of pathetic poor person.

And while we're on the topic of heat, the only way to get past it is to jump in the lake or a pool and listen to your skin sizzle like a plate of fajitas.

How everyone here is afraid of gay people, except for people who are actually gay, in which case they are afraid of everyone else.

Giant HEB grocery stores that confuse the heck out of me now that I have gotten used to little ol' Trader Joe's.

But, like I said, I have to dwell on these negativities to keep myself from craving so much Texas goodness once I go home to San Francisco.

Deep in my Texan heart I truly miss the many unique eccentricities of my home state, which often lives up to its little tourist motto of resembling a "whole 'nother country." I even feel a sort of kinship with the Texas Alamo hero, Mr. Davy Crockett, who said:

"You may all go to hell and I will go to TEXAS!"

Free Seventy-Two Ounce Steak If Eaten in One Hour

Now that I'm a mom, I often experience an intense solidarity with my own mother's rare acceptance of corn syrup, sodium, and partially hydrogenated crap as a substitute for real food. She forced us to snack on fruit, to drink the dreaded water, and to eat our veggies. However, on occasion we were allowed to shun the regular nutritional rules and eat like goats.

These occasions, our frequent road trips, are often replayed in memory with Willie Nelson's "On the Road Again" as the omnipresent theme song. Classic country musicians, like Waylon Jennings, Johnny Cash and Willie would croon about hard drinking and heartaches from the eight-track tape player of my parents' wood-paneled station wagon, and I would eat junk food across the state of Texas.

Most of the time we visited my grandparents in the Texas Panhandle, in a small town called Borger. My parents grew up in Borger, high school sweeties who found love under the haze of the nearby oil refinery. They remained close to their families even as they migrated down the Panhandle to the oil country of Midland. We made a pilgrimage back to Borger so regularly that we developed a well-honed road trip routine, and what I saw and ate along the Lone Star highways shaped much of my girlhood.

We never passed what I called a "real" farm as we negotiated the straight, flat plains. The West Texas sun mainly nurtured tumbleweeds, cattle, and cactus. I mostly observed rows and rows of cotton lining the highway. The orderly lines of plants would morph into an optical illusion as we rushed by, reminding me of the spokes on my bicycle, spinning, dizzily in the bright sunlight.

Before we got to Lubbock, our official lunch stop, we always took a potty break in Lamesa, at the Mary Ann's Convenience Store. I would buy a small box of Cheese-Its, a can of Big Red, and an Archie comic book. Years of road trip comics gave me a warped view of buxom, Barbie-ish high schoolers as the standard of beauty. The comparisons often left me feeling sub-par— Betty and Veronica were hot, and they definitely did not have my hair and pigmentation.

Lubbock meant lunch. We usually grabbed greasy burgers somewhere near the Texas Tech University campus, my parents' alma mater. I loved the excessively out-of-ordinary permission to gorge myself on fast food when we stopped to stretch our legs and eliminate our sugary drinks. My sister, Lara, and I humored Dad and listened to the story about the-time-the-alligator-escaped-in-a-building-on-campus-during-college for the fiftieth time. Mom gushed romantically about their days of newlywed poverty at Tech, struggling to finish school with the menacing shadow of Viet Nam lurking around the corner. We had heard it all before, but we loved to ponder the rehashed impossibility that our parents had lives before we existed.

By the time we drove through Amarillo, the sugar and caffeine buzz began to fade, and I became too weary to play our favorite license plate game. Instead I trained my laser-like focus on the on the horizon, waiting for the four-story neon and metal cowboy with the sign that says,

FREE SEVENTY-TWO OUNCE STEAK IF EATEN IN ONE HOUR.

"Please pull over Dad! I need to try to win that free steak!" I yelled from the backseat.

"Do you even know how big a seventy-two ounce steak is?" my mother craned her neck from the front seat and stared down at me.

"Uh-uh."

"It's probably the size of our entire kitchen table. You only eat one or two ounces of steak at home."

I mentally constructed the kind of person who could devour a slab of meat that might take up more space than my own skinny little body. I came up with a grizzled trucker wearing a ball cap that said "TAKE THIS JOB AND SHOVE IT." His flannel shirt strained tightly across a globular belly, which hung over the top of Wrangler jeans. He wore an enormous napkin tied around his neck, and when he finished the humungous piece of meat he would lean back, belch, and pick his teeth with a matchstick pulled from behind his ear. I had seen enough men like this at various Dairy Queens between Midland and Borger. He wasn't hard to imagine.

Even though my mom warned me about the massive size of the steak, I refused to let a road trip go by without pressing the issue. I had never won a spelling bee nor excelled in athletics. The opportunity for local notoriety reached out to this competitive little girl and shook her by the pigtails.

Convinced that I could be eating gratis on each trip to Borger, I meticulously planned my meat-winning strategy as if I were the proverbial tortoise beating the hare. I would start the slab slowly then hurry to finish the final bits of flesh by the end of the hour. In this fantasy, I faced worthy opponents: the afore-mentioned truck driver, an enormous trailer park resident with curlers in her hair, and the winner of the Texas State Fair pie-eating contest. But my wit and cunning would ultimately put me on top. I fantasized wearing my "I won the free 72 ounce steak" ribbon, as if there was such a thing, to school the following Monday, earning much respect and admiration from my less-abled peers.

Alas, my folks refused to relent, and each trip to Borger left me staring out the rear window of the wagon, watching the giant metal cowboy and his companion, a red and white RV-sized steer, fade into the distance.

Once we passed the steak cowboy, the ride to Borger seemed interminable, and by the time we got to Nana's house I was dizzy with hunger. I would run through her front door, tear across the living room of her shotgun house and make like an arrow for the ceramic apple-shaped cookie jar. I forgot all about the uneaten monster steak and stuffed myself with Nana's famous chocolate chip cookies. They were the final sugary payoff for the six hours of fluctuating hyperactivity and boredom.

The most vivid recollections of my childhood road trips belong to the food, gluttonous treats that were strictly off-limits in the real world that existed off the highway: lukewarm cans of soda; half-eaten bags of Oreo's crunched under the car seat; Dairy Queen chili dogs; packets of orange crackers encasing petrified peanut butter; Dad's covert bags of peanut M & M's, hidden in his lap; Nana's cookies; and of course, the ever-elusive giant steak. Being "on the road," with Willie warbling in the background, allowed us to drop the daily food pyramid and go straight for the garbage. I found comfort and safety in the rhythm and predictability of my fatty, salty, caffeinated goodies, even in my never-realized, carnivorous fantasy.

These days I often find that I sound just like my mom, futilely trying to convince my daughter that the extra jelly beans just aren't a good idea. But sometimes, during lengthy car rides, I catch a glimpse of her little face in the rearview mirror and I see myself as a child. I recall the boredom and excitement of travel and that in-between space in which everyday rules are suspended. I remember how I eagerly looked forward to each trip to Borger where I wallowed in a kid-fantasy food high, just seventy-two ounces short of nirvana.

And when this happens, I pop in the Willie Nelson CD and pass back the cookies.

Big Sister's House

"Mommy, is our house new?"

"No. It's very, very old. Probably one-hundred years old."

"Oh. Is Angelica's house new?" my daughter asked, referring to a mama-friend.

"No. It is old too. Maybe even older than our house."

"Oh." Thoughtful pause. "Well, I want a house like Angelica's."

"What does Angelica's house have that makes you want a house like that?"

Another thoughtful pause. "It has a big sister in it."

CRASH!

It is difficult to transcribe the sound of my heart shattering into a thousand broken pieces. But I think I may have audibly heard such a noise that afternoon as Grace and I puttered around the kitchen.

I declined to respond directly to her subtle request for a sister, unsure of how to tell her that her daddy and I have been trying desperately to help her *be* the coveted big sister. Instead of revealing our fertility traumas, so well-concealed for the past several months, I just hugged her close and said, "That's so sweet. It must be fun to have a big sister. We'll tell Angelica you said that."

The conversation moved on to the muffins we were making, but her words haunted me. Grace has definitely noticed that most of her little friends have siblings and that most of those siblings come in the form of new babies. Grace goes nuts over babies, slobbering her dolls and the real flesh-and-blood sibs of her friends alike in mounds of kisses and grimy hugs.

Sometimes when we say good-bye to good friends after a playdate, Grace gives more attention to the infant sister of her pal than to her fellow three-year-old. After our buddies leave, Grace will gather her own precious mass-produced Baby Chou Chou in her arms and calmly sit on the sofa, cuddling the baby. Grace leans her chubby cheeks down to rub her nose against the doll's synthetic face and whisper sweet secrets only meant for Chou Chou's ears. Then she pulls up her own shirt and holds the baby tight to "nurse."

On a good day, these scenes evoke a poignant smile at my daughter's charming ability to play such a nurturing game of make-believe. On a bad day, they evoke stinging tears of irony as they remind me of my own womb's recent cruel inability to retain a new fetus for longer than eight weeks.

The first miscarriage wasn't so bad. More like a heavy period. The second miscarriage offered blood and pain of mythic proportions, forcing me to take to the bed for three days to bleed and hurt and cry. They were the loneliest, most traumatic three days of my life, but we successfully shielded Grace from the trauma by telling her Mama was in bed with a bellyache.

And now, recovered from the pain and the blood, I am working on the fear, the loss, the grief of "letting go." I am letting go of my plans, my expectations, my smug confidence in my own body's ability to do whatever I ask. I am a walking cliché, a poster child for pop-Buddhist wisdom on Being Here Now, Living in the Present, and Taking It One Day at a Time. I personify the tired old adage of Life Being What Happens When You Are Busy Making Plans.

I find myself bonding anew with my best friend from college. Separated by an entire continent, we have both recently nursed losses of potential. We have both dragged ourselves in circles over what might have been. The phone calls, with their three-hour time differences stretched from Brooklyn to San Francisco, flood forth our trite clichés with an earnestness only appreciated by those who grieve.

Despite of all of this grief, I still clutch at hope. Just recently, the sight of a giant pregnant woman no longer made me want to scream. Instead, I smiled, reveling in that shared insider knowledge that all mamas quietly transmit to one another when the moment is right.

I've been where you are. I know what you are going through.
And I have faith that I will be there again.
And then our house will be like Angelica's. It will have a big sister.

Soul Shoes

"I like your shoes!" proclaimed an enthusiastic fellow mother outside of the children's art studio.

"Thanks." I looked down at my paisley-patterned, thong sandals. "They're really old," I added.

This brief exchange, a respite from herding our three-year-olds around the tables of the delightfully grubby art class, got me thinking about my well-worn sandals.

Now, to old timers who may have hung on to a prom dress for forty years, a thirteen-year-old pair of patterned Birkenstocks may seem like the spring chickens of footwear. But for a thirtysomething like me, someone born and bred to consume and toss, these shoes could qualify for a prime spot in a Gen X museum.

My gizeh-model Birkenstocks were originally purchased on Guadalupe Street (the Drag) in Austin at a crunchy-granola, earth-mama shoe store. They have since been packed in more moving boxes and suitcases than I can count. They have traipsed up and down both coasts of the U.S., plus Hawaii. They have been to Europe, Mexico and the Caribbean.

They were worn to early morning undergraduate women's studies classes, accompanied by a loose sundress and a hangover. They clomped through muddy fields to hear Pearl Jam (before the "comeback") and Lollapalooza (back when Jane's Addiction still headlined.) They epitomized early 90s Seattle grunge meets Phish show parking lot attire.

When I got my first grown-up job, the sandals stayed with me on the weekend. I slid tired feet into their curved embrace after a busy evening shaking hands with a load of mucky-mucks at a fancy work dinner. I wore them out to a boat party, where well-paid attorneys pretended they were still young and crazy and jumped, naked, into the waters of Lake Austin.

The sandals stayed with me as I went west to Arizona, then on to California. They fell out of fashion for a while, especially with the Phoenix stiletto heel/fake tan set. But I couldn't let them go.

They accompanied me on a spree of DINK (that's Dual-Income-No-Kids) living with my spouse, as we traveled, dined and spent with wild abandon.

These shoes supported swollen ankles, an aching back and the enormous belly of pregnancy. Their gentle support lifted me up on days when the growing child inside me seemed to weigh me down like a stone in my gut.

My sandals caressed my tired tootsies after hours of pacing the floor with a confused and wailing newborn. They pounded miles and miles of San Francisco concrete, supporting a baby-filled sling or an overloaded stroller. They've chased a toddler, and now a preschooler, through sandpits, up and over playground structures, and around the merry-go-round.

My old sandals have seen college keg puke and baby breastmilk vomit. I've accidentally peed on them by the side of the road in a camping emergency, and I've accidentally dropped a dirty diaper on them. These shoes have shopped in high end Union Square department stores and been filled with the filthiest playground sand in Northern California.

Last summer, with the whole Boho chic thing all the rage, I started seeing my sandals pop up everywhere. Suddenly my comfy staples were cool again. The dear old things hadn't had a compliment in years and now they are graced with praises of their beauty each time they leave the house.

They've still got it.

I wish that I could say I've aged as well as this pair of sandals. And maybe I have. They're sturdy and solid. They definitely have some wear around the edges, but they retain a nice superficial beauty if you don't look too close. They are rugged and do their job well. They are dependable, loyal and not too flashy.

Someday they'll wear out or else they'll succumb, once again, to the random ebb and flow of fashion. Until then, I'll take any compliments I can get.

Confessions of a Wedding Coordinator

One of the many squares in what my family affectionately refers to as my "quilt of jobs," is that of Wedding Coordinator at my church.

This square fits in nicely alongside other quilt squares of full-time mom, survey evaluator, poseur-writer-who-is-desperate-for-a-break, and professional laundress. (The last one is a joke. I am a not-for-profit laundress.)

Yes, as a Wedding Coordinator, I am the J-Lo of a certain liberal church in the very liberal City of San Francisco.

If you know anything about San Francisco church-goers, you know that this means that instead of wearing stilettos and a pink suit that accentuates my Lloyd's of London-insured derriere, I wear loose trousers and a pair of Dankso clogs. Instead of rushing around in a self-important fuss, barking orders into my state-of-the art headset while pounding my palm pilot, I gently guide the wedding party through a series of meditations designed to embrace all cultures, races, languages, and sexual orientations. Church is a little more laid-back around here.

But the effect is the same. My job is to help the bride, the groom and, the most important member of the wedding party, the Mother of the Bride, to have a smooth, memorable nuptial experience.

This part-time gig provides a vital link in the ongoing effort to help my small family remain above the poverty level in a city where the cost of rent alone could (and I'm not exaggerating here) feed a small country for several months. Or else buy one heck of a luxury car for your landlord.

When I first took the job, I also reasoned that helping people pull off their weddings would assist in the racking up of some major good karma points.

I figured that, in terms of feel-good material, being a Wedding Coordinator would rank up alongside assisting at births and helping people to rid their CD collection of unwanted Van Halen discs from the Sammy Hagar era.

I was right about the karma bit. And I have had the added benefit of continuing my lifelong need for education and enrichment. In case any of you readers are interested in becoming a Wedding Coordinator, I encourage you to clip and save this handy list of tips and hints I have gleaned thus far in my endeavor.

Advice for the beginning Wedding Coordinator:

If you are nervous about gaining the respect of the bride, the groom, the wedding party, and the Exalted Almighty Mother of the Bride, be sure to carry a clipboard. As Dave Barry once said, it is hard to argue with a woman who carries a clipboard.

There is a little known theory of physics (and I double checked with my physics-teacher-father-in-law on this one) stating that the number of children in a wedding party has a ratio that is in inverse proportion to the resilience of the sanctuary walls to absorb requests to go pee-pee during the ceremony.

If the father of the bride is an 8th grade P.E. coach then you best sit down, shut up and pay attention. Do you hear me, People?!

When initially approaching the Mother of the Bride do not be frightened. Keep your head down and do not make eye-contact until you have assessed the situation to be safe. Extend your hand in what is commonly known in Western culture as a polite, submissive greeting. Do not show an abundance of teeth when you smile, as it can be interpreted as a sign of aggression and result in wads of to-do lists being shoved in various orifices.

All seemingly humorous requests by groomsmen to place kegs in the choir loft should be taken quite seriously.

In keeping with the above warning, remember that bridesmaids' dresses should never be the object of stifled laughter. Unless the bride specifically indicates that it is an 80s-themed wedding do not make the mistake of informing the wedding party that Madonna called and she wants her *Like a Virgin* Tour wardrobe back.

Another wedding etiquette tip I learned the hard way: always refrain from asking the bride if she is Mail-Order or Regular. And while we're on the subject, do not presume to know the gender of either the bride or groom. (This is San Francisco, after all.)

Wedding photographers are generally very creepy people who invariably develop a crush on an unsuspecting bridesmaid, cousin or Wedding Coordinator. Try to keep your head down and out of un-posed photos or else you may end up on someone's fetish website.

It is often necessary to shepherd the less technologically savvy members of the ministerial staff. Unless you want the entire congregation to hear the bathroom behavior of the Reverend, be sure to turn off his or her wireless microphone until right before the ceremony starts.

Bridesmaids tend to lock their knees. This can lead to one or more of the women passing out and causing a scene that distracts from the beauty and serenity of the moment. To prevent such disasters, I recommend that all bridesmaids drink lots and lots of white wine before the ceremony to keep their knees loose.

If, by the end of the wedding, the Mother of the Bride has not passed out from anxiety and fatigue you may politely assist in this process via the distribution of Nytol, vodka or a combination of the above.

Beyond this, I learned that, no matter what happens, all weddings are beautiful. No matter how many crises or problems occur, at the end of the day two people have joined their lives together in a momentous union. I learned that if I have done my job well as the Wedding Coordinator I should be invisible, just a forgotten behind-the-scenes player who evaporates like the mist of so many champagne bubbles once the Big Day is over.

I also learned to always check the microphone before the minister heads to the bathroom.

Preschool Chronicles: No Shoots Allowed

It's the great social experiment: pushing your child out of the nest and standing back to watch what happens. In other words, it's preschool. And I'm in the thick of an experience common to many parents of preschoolers.

I'm not talking about missing my baby. Or adjusting to life in the carpool lane. Or worrying about what to do with my time during those long, empty, luxurious, heavenly hours, when I am lucky enough to have them.

I'm talking about learning to accept that I am no longer the final authority on all things my child may be exposed to in this nutty world.

I present, for example, a rough-and-tumble after school moment we had last week.

"I'm going to poke you in the eye with a sword!"

My nurturing daughter, who loves nothing better than to walk around the house pretending to nurse her toy babies and tuck them into bed, suddenly threatened me like a *Mortal Combat* aficionado!

"Excuse me? We don't poke people in the eyes in this house. That is against our House Rules." I snapped back. *And where the heck did she learn about a sword?* I thought. *No doubt from those wild boys who run around like pro-wrestlers on the playground.*

Our "house rules" tend to be a bit flexible. Jeff and I often make up rules on the spot. We have gems such as House Rule #273, "No yelling or playing with the remote control while the Longhorns play football," and House Rule #17, "No eating crackers in the living room unless it's already really dirty and needs to be vacuumed anyway."

But, "NOBODY HITS ANYBODY" is inarguably House Rule #1 in our as-yet unwritten domestic Magna Carta.

"Mia has rules too. She says no shoots allowed in her classroom." Grace retorted.

"What is 'shoots'?"

"It's like this." She pointed her finger at my chest and made a *PKOW* sound. *Oh Lord*, I thought, *it's the gun thing. Where did she pick up that one? We never talk about guns!*

At least she didn't jack her thumb up, gun-style. Yet. I'm sure she'll learn it next week.

"That's a good rule. We don't play shoots in our house, either," I said.

I grew up around guns and, as I have previously mentioned, both my father and my uncle have lost digits in hunting accidents. I also live in an urban area where teenagers tragically take each other out with guns almost every week. I have a healthy respect for (and fear of) guns and I'll stick to my, er, guns on this one.

I let the weapons issue go, not wanting to devote too much attention to the violent new games. I wondered what else my daughter was "learning" at preschool.

Then the other day in the car, out of nowhere I heard a little voice pipe up. "Mama. I want a Darth Vaver doll for Christmas."

"What's Darth Vaver?"

"He's a scary guy that's on grown-up TV."

"I don't think they make Darth Vaver dolls," I white-lied thinking about my own figurine. "Hey look at that fire truck!" And the subject was dropped. For now. But I quietly lamented this loss of innocence, and the cold-hard truth that Anakin Skywalker's evil alter-ego would inevitably return.

I drove on, feeling sad that my little girl was only three-and-a-half and already the rough outside world threatened to undo the foundation of peace and non-violence we were desperately trying to build under her. What should I do? More time in church? Less TV? More books? All of the above?

But, of course, there is an upside to of all this socialization outside the protective confines of the family.

"Does Joey speak Rosh Hashanah at his house?" Grace inquired one night at the dinner table. I mentally scanned through my three-year-old translation manual—a resource familiar to many parents. Ummm…was she asking if her friend is Jewish?

"Do you mean does he speak Russian?" I finally deciphered.

"Yea! That! What you said!"

"I think Joey speaks Czech. Natasha speaks Russian." *How cool, is that?* I thought. *My little English-speaking Caucasian girl already notices so many languages!*

I spent the rest of the evening bursting with pride at my daughter's ability to tune in to her richly diverse classroom, full of languages and colors. I realized that Grace's best girlfriends at preschool are Japanese-American, Russian-American and African-American.

Another side effect of preschool has been a cognitive growth spurt like that of a small baby. Every day Grace demonstrates a new style of drawing, adding hair and feet to her people or learning to scribble enough colors to cover an entire sheet of paper. She wants to know new words in Spanish. She has an obsession with counting EVERYTHING she sees, and a leaning toward actual math. She constantly writes words, working on her letters and wanting to know how to spell.

I can't say if all of this crazy brain activity is a direct by-product of her incredibly stimulating preschool room or only a coincidence. But she's happy and I'll take it. Even if it means we have to shoots Darth Vaver.

A Beastly Blessing

We left the main section of the hiking path shortly after the Ranger talk. I'd had about enough of waddling tourists throwing chewed-up gum into the underbrush of the mammoth redwoods – more than I would have been able to stand during a non-pregnant time. I realized that day on our hike through Muir Woods, a mystical park of old growth Redwoods about twenty minutes north of San Francisco, that my expectant-mama hormones unfortunately exacerbated my level of intolerance. I furrowed my brow in a long-suffering grimace as I loped past the dawdling crowd. Rather than slow me down, the child in my belly seemed to propel me forward, away from the throngs of people and into what I deemed "real" nature.

"Let's go up here!" I yelled back at my husband, Jeff, and my sister, Lara. "Away from the crowded part!"

I scurried up a ledge, away from most of the hikers, and into the deep quiet of Muir Woods. The new trail, although clearly marked, was no longer covered in the eco-friendly wooden boardwalk that denoted the oft-traveled area. The dirt path we now trod upon snaked in and out of deep shadows and sparkling shafts of yellow, cutting through the towering ancient trees. I turned around, breathing hard already, and saw a religious-postcard swath of sunlight streak across Jeff's bronze skin.

He'll be a *Daddy* soon, I thought, and paused to let the other two hikers catch up.

The trip to Muir Woods was a respite from recent chaos. Jeff and I had moved to San Francisco on a Monday and found out we were pregnant with Grace on Friday. I dug the pregnancy test out of a moving box full of bathroom supplies yet to be unpacked. It was positive. This news of impending parenthood threw us into frenzy: new jobs, new apartment, new progressive urban city, and new life about to join us. After we became somewhat settled in, my sister came out from Texas to distract me from the stress that threatened to overwhelm me at times. We all traveled across the Golden Gate Bridge to visit the primeval trees of Muir Woods. The forest, in turn, welcomed me out of my recent urban whirlwind, wrapping me and the growing life inside me in its cool embrace.

As the three of us hiked deeper into the woods, I came across a silence like nothing I've experienced before or since. It can best be compared to the quiet of a deep cavern. Although we human visitors were surrounded by nature, there was nothing of the usual cacophony of chirps, whirrs, tweets and twitters. Because the Redwoods so effectively block out the sun from the ground below, no birds or insects live in Muir Woods. This lack of bustling life creates an ethereal quiet that, combined with the skyscraper-sized trees, evokes a feeling of holy space. Once Jeff, Lara and I moved away from the shuffling crowds and stopped chatting to each other, the silence swallowed our small hiking party. We moved in tandem, yet each of us seemed isolated in our own world. It was a feeling akin to a group prayer or meditation, appropriate for these woods considered sacred by Native people.

We ambled along, cognizant of the only sounds coming from the gentle crunch of our boots on the gravel beneath our feet. Our trail followed along the edge of a small hill, dropping off sharply into a ravine with a river at the bottom. Across the river, the ground rose up just as steep, so that I could look across a span of twenty yards and see the roots of old growth Redwoods at eye level.

"Remember when Emery took that trip to Alaska?" I said, breaking the silence to reference Jeff's outdoorsy little brother. "Where they had to learn what to do if one of them got eaten by a bear?"

"Ooh! Watch out! A bear!" On cue, my husband started clowning around. He waved his arms around in mock bear-stance, further shattering the calm, beautiful silence with our human intrusion. Of course, he didn't really see anything. Or did he?

In one of those coincidences deemed too uncanny to be anything else, I suddenly registered a slight rustling on the hill across the river from us. I jerked my head up and saw brown fur moving in the bushes.

Holy shit it really is a bear, was all I could think.

I was paralyzed, immobile in my discovery of a dangerous wild animal less than twenty yards away. The creature lifted its head and I saw that it wasn't a bear. It was a huge mountain lion. And it met my gaze directly, its yellow eyes peering out of a white-haloed face.

We stared at each other, the lion and I. Time froze. The phrase "never been so scared" does little justice to the adrenaline cocktail that sluiced through my veins.   I felt a weakening between my legs, as if the muscles in my pelvic floor had lost their function and morphed into jelly. I didn't fully urinate on myself, but I at once understood how fear could cause this reaction. My belly clenched involuntarily around the growing child inside, threatening to lurch right up and out of my suddenly unbearably dry throat. Having nursed in irrational fear of sharks since childhood (a result of an exposure to the movie *Jaws* at far too impressionable an age) it would not have surprised me to have such a reaction to a face-to-face meeting with a wild beast in the water. But my primal, innate response to the big cat caught me off guard.

I broke the animal's gaze, then turned and started to walk quickly in the other direction. My protective-mama hormones were infused with a healthy dose of fight-or-flight instinct. "Let's go! NOW!" I barked at my sister and husband.

In a flash Lara understood the sound of fear emanating from her big sister. "What?" she yelled, frozen behind me. "What? WHAT? WHAT? What's going on?" I looked back and saw that her eyes were wild, obviously picking up on my terror. Jeff stood by Lara, staring at me incredulously.

"Please!" I whined. "Just hurry." In my fear, I lost the ability to articulate the object of my terror, as if the mountain lion might somehow hear me and decide to leap across the ravine and plow his jaws into my tender belly. A vision of the beast on top of Jeff or Lara suddenly blazed through my imagination.

Oh my God! What will I do if it leaps on one of them? I frantically scanned the ground, still running, for a large rock or branch, something I could use to beat the creature should it attack a loved one. In a split second I realized that, should the animal decide to attack, it would probably go for the throat, ripping the jugular and killing the victim instantly.

"Please hurry!" I looked over my shoulder and intoned again. Finally they were behind me. I ran until we got back to the well-populated trail that had annoyed me earlier, grateful to be surrounded by the perceived safety of a crowd. By the time Lara and Jeff caught up to me they were beyond freaked out.

"Did you see a pervert in the woods or something?" Jeff panted.

"No. A Mountain Lion."

"Damn! I want to see it!" Lara turned and started to head back to the trail.

"Yeah, me too. Can we go back?" asked Jeff.

Still physically shaking, I nearly burst into tears. "Are you kidding?" I clutched each of their arms like I could somehow physically restrain them. "I can't let either of you get eaten! I can't get eaten! I am going to be a mama! I have to take care of myself!"

"Are you sure you saw a mountain lion?" Jeff put his hands on his hips.

"Hell yes, I'm sure! Do you think I could fake this?" I held out my hand and showed him my quivering fingers. "Let's go tell the park ranger."

After several group hugs and pleas for me to calm down, we wandered back to the gift shop. Jeff and Lara grumbled the whole way that I didn't tell them about the cat in time for them to see it. When we told the ranger about my face-off with the lion his face fell in a genuine display of jealousy. No one seemed to understand how bad the experience had shaken me.

Later that week I called my friend Samantha and told her the whole story. Sam, who worked for the park service near Muir Woods and spent her days deep in the world of reforestation, had a different reaction.

"You know, Robin," she said. "People work in the woods of Northern California for thirty years and never see a mountain lion. I think this is a blessing. It is a gift, a sign that your baby will be strong and hearty, and maybe a little wild, just like a lion."

Her words, even over the phone, washed over me like a shot of something stronger than I usually like to drink. And I felt a stillness and peace about the child inside me. My fears about building a family in our new city, in the midst of so much change, gently subsided. Perhaps I was meant to see that wild beast, as I was meant to hear Sam's words to calm the beasts of fear that kept me awake so many nights.

Years later, my child is now strong and hearty, and a little wild, just like a lion. Jeff and I have taken her to Muir Woods, but we have yet to see a mountain lion again. We have tried very hard to have another child, with no success yet and a string of heartbreaking miscarriages. Often, in my grief over these losses, I have stopped and considered the meaning I derived from my mountain lion sighting as an omen. I have even gone so far as to wonder if Jeff's initial assumption was right and I hallucinated the whole thing. Whether or not I did is irrelevant, for the personal meaning that I have assigned to the vision is what matters. My memory of the mountain lion is a reminder of the fragility and wonder of all existence, the miracle of each new beginning and the reality of our tenuous grasp on it all. It is a reminder to be thankful for my beautiful child, for she is a blessing from Nature.

33 Ways I Know I'm An Adult

1. I'm 33 years old. That's old. Really old.
2. I am a mother. It is automatic adulthood, no matter what your age.
3. I get a hangover if I have two drinks in a two hour span.
4. As one of my best college girlfriends said, "We all have grown-up problems now." (Marriage crises, miscarriages, deaths)
5. I color my gray hairs.
6. I have sore feet and prescription inserts for my sneakers
7. I wore all the clothes that the teenagers wear today...back when I was a teenager in the 80s.
8. 7:30 a.m. is considered sleeping late.
9. My obsessive fear of sharks been replaced with more realistic obsessive fears that I'd rather not go into right now.
10. I RSVP and write thank you notes.
11. I'd rather open a bottle of wine than take a shot.
12. I don't fight with my sister...well, we don't fight as much as we used to.
13. Grudges weigh more these days. They're harder to carry around.
14. My cesarean scar is much larger and more interesting than my bicycle crash scar.
15. I listen more and better and longer.
16. When a 40-year-old dude flirts with me, I smile and feel flattered rather than snarl at the nasty old pervert.
17. I laugh at *The Office* because I have enough work history to personally know each and every character on that show.
18. I no longer wear overalls.

19. I own at least one of each of the following: black interview suit, black heels, tasteful black cocktail dress, black pantyhose, black leather notebook, fancy black pen, professional black carryall.
20. I have stuffed all of the above items in the back of the closet because I spend most of my days with a small child or hunched over a computer in my pajamas.
21. Sunscreen is mandatory and applied daily to all members of my household.
22. I know how to use a recipe other than the instructions on the back of the macaroni and cheese box.
23. Since when did college students get so young?
24. And what about the slutty clothes that teenagers wear these days?
25. My daughter and I are each 15 years away from age 18.
26. I worry about access to birth control. But not for me...for the next generation.
27. I no longer have fantasies about my college professors.
28. I am married to a college professor.
29. I am on the cusp of not relating to any of the material in *Jane* magazine.
30. I sorta dig *Good Housekeeping* (but only for the recipes!)
31. Rather than just complain, I try to actually do something about my peeve of the week.
32. I willingly eat all manner of dark, leafy greens.
33. I go to church, not because my parents make me, but because I want to.

And a few ways I'm still not quite an adult:

1. I call my mommy for advice.
2. A surprise picture of a gape-mouthed Great White shark will still invoke a yet-to-be-dealt-with early childhood trauma resulting from the movie *Jaws*.
3. I ask my dad for money.
4. No second home, (no first home), no mortgage, no property taxes, no equity. (Yes, we rent.)
5. I sometimes wear pigtails.
6. Macaroni and cheese is a dinnertime (and lunchtime and breakfast-time) staple.
7. I unleash my inner teenage anarchist by making a zine.
8. I make obsessive lists in lieu of doing any actual work.

Is it Chili in Here, or Is It Me?

Every year around this time, my Dad locks himself in the kitchen for a few days and whips up a batch of his famous deer meat chili. He cooks several different pots of the stuff, with varying levels of spice. The mildest version, the one that Dad calls "tomato soup", is gentle on the sensitive stomach of my petite and temperate Nana. The other end of the gastric continuum offers a blistering blend of peppers and spices that will melt the fillings in your teeth.

When my Dad gets going on the chili, accidents are frequent and spectacular. Once, I waltzed into the kitchen only to bust my father singing along with Johnny Cash while he stirred the saucepot with a bloody rag wrapped around his dripping hand. He had just chopped himself with a paring knife and was having too good a time to stop cooking and get a band-aid.

Our most talked-about chili catastrophe is definitely the time when Daddy dropped an extra-large vat of his extra-spicy recipe across the kitchen floor, setting a household record for world's longest chili trail. The lumpy burnt sienna chili made a path down the front of Dad's body, whooshed across the linoleum, streaked up the opposite wall, and finally halted when it splashed across the ceiling.

"Shhhhhhhhhhhhheeeeeeeeeeeeeeeeiiiiiiiiiiiit!"

My Dad's anguished cry, a primordial bellow that can best be compared to Walt Whitman's barbaric yawp, echoed across our cul-de-sac, rattling car windows and nerves for miles. Ever the entrepreneurial kids, my sister and I coasted on about a year's worth of "but Daddy said it," from this one slip of the S-word.

When I tell some of my native Bay Area friends about Dad's venison meat chili, and how he gathers the main ingredient on his big macho hunting trips, they usually open their eyes wide in amazement. But that's nothing compared to their reactions to the story of my Dad and his brother each shooting off digits on said deer hunting trips.

Yes, I shall finally lay it all out for you.

On two separate occasions my uncle and father each played the role of well-meaning, safety-conscious deer hunters who made disastrous blunders and lost a finger and a toe, respectively. My Uncle, who is a dentist and a sculptor, had obvious professional ramifications from the loss of his middle finger, but he was fortunate enough to regain a surgically created digit thanks to some borrowed skin and bone from other parts of his body.

Dad's toe had a less happy ending. He and some hunting buddies were hanging out in a cabin on a deer lease outside of Beeville, Texas, when Dad's shotgun went off and blew the end of his boot clean to god-knows-where. His poor little second toe was lost in the madness.

One family theory holds that, amid the chaos of the accident, one of Dad's co-hunters threw the toe out the front door and a coyote ate it. We also like to grossly speculate that perhaps a little bit of Dad-meat got mixed up with the take from that day's hunt.

Later, when Dad finally got all of the bandages off and my sister and I were able to have a look at what we now call the "No Toe," we recoiled in horror at the new alien foot sprouting from the end of his leg. Of course, we soon got used to the odd appearance of Dad's lowest appendage, but I always delight in describing the mutant foot to anyone who will listen.

So listen up. My Dad's second toe is now permanently missing in action, and a deep, v-shaped wedge drives down the length of his foot in the space between his big and middle toes. The whole thing arches into a nasty curve, reminiscent of a demon hand from a bad 70's horror film. This odd-shaped foot serves as excellent entertainment for my three-year-old daughter, who still can't quite wrap her head around why her Bob-o's toes only go up to number nine.

And, sadly, at this point Dad has now rid himself of all thirteen pairs of his exotic-leather cowboy boots, as his curled and misshapen foot no longer fit in them. But you can bet your NRA membership that the loss of one little toe doesn't stop him from heading out to the hunting lease as soon as he gathers up his yearly deer-shootin' license.

And on each Christmas Eve, my family still reflects on Dad's good fortune in the face of such a horrific accident, grateful that the only loss was one little toe. We continue to gather around the deer meat chili and praise our family's patriarch for heroically harvesting our dinner from wild herds of ferocious deer. We always offer both silent and vocal prayers of gratitude that we are all healthy and whole.

Well, almost whole. Minus one toe.

Loose Ends

We're all at loose ends here. A series of viruses trailed my family on the heels of the holidays. The house has yet to recover from the Christmas explosion. And we've been dealing with a few other things that are either too personal or too, well, *personal* to go into in this fluffy bit of space.

I don't have the brainpower or the physical energy to string together a coherent thought with a beginning, middle, and end. But I have been gathering a small collection of mini-insights, a sort of medley of musings based on a few observations in my house of late. I doubt I could stretch any of these bad boys out into anything longer than a few paragraphs, but if I squish all of these thoughts together in a haphazard list, you might get something resembling an insight. At least let's pretend that is the case and move on.

Without further ado, I present some *Foggiest Idea* errata:

The spicy vagina.

I'll get the risqué bit over with up front. My child frequently bellows from the bathroom that indeed, her lady parts feel a wee bit on the uncomfortable side. Aside from the fact that this oft-heard, three-year-old saying, "My vagina is spicy!" gives me the willies, it also causes gasps of shock from certain listeners of more genteel breeding, such as, oh let's say MY MOTHER.

We have been working like mad to teach my daughter to use the word "chapped" to describe her delicate nether regions, all the while struggling equally to keep a straight face.

Why do old people love *Happy Feet*?

Before you take offense to the term "old" (dear Mom and Mother-in-law) please know that this is a quote from my buddy Kim, who referred to her own octogenarian in-laws with the question in consideration after they practically traded the deed to their house in exchange for a chance to take their granddaughter to this show.

In fact, every friend of mine who has a child under the age of five spent her holidays fending off (or giving into) the requests, nay, the pleas of grandparents to escort said child to the movie *Happy Feet*. Of course, the initial reaction is to assume that the sweetie grandparents were just looking for an excuse to bond with their little grandchild over the most innocuous film on the market in December. After all, what were the alternatives, *Apocalypto* or *Saw III*?

But my husband, Jeff, thinks there was something sharper at work there. Jeff firmly believes that a motivated junior executive at Warner Brothers really tested the movie on Baby Boomer grandparents, knowing they would loot their well-earned retirement accounts on *Happy Feet* swag once proper marketing saturation had been achieved. Remember what teenage girls did for *Titanic*?

The Fancy-fication of my neighborhood

Every morning in my neighborhood it's the same story. The Mercedes station wagons and the Lexus SUVs pull out of the driveways, and the pickup trucks full of contractors and day laborers pull in. As soon as their lattes have cooled, the real estate agents roar along in their convertible BMW roadsters and tricked-out Range Rovers.

Houses are being ripped apart, gutted, refurbished, spit-polished, and dressed up in their Sunday finest. Then they are being sold for more money than most hard-working Americans will ever see in a lifetime.

I have learned to navigate the neighborhood more skillfully than Ricky Bobby, dodging orange cones and building permit signs on each block. Our 'hood, once full of blue-collar families of cops and plumbers, now teems with Google and Yahoo zillionares who pay $1 million for a two-bedroom tear down. The stores are getting fancier too. The cutesy ice cream shop is closed, replaced by a five-buck-a-cup gelateria. (By the way, "gelateria" is so fancy that it surpasses the ability of my computer's spellcheck.)

Our neighborhood is so fancy that I sometimes feel like I no longer fit in, but the thought of moving makes me want to crawl up and hibernate inside one of the hundreds of worker port-a-potties that line our streets. I guess I'll tough it out and try to fake it 'til we make it.

There is a new person living in our house.

My husband and I first became aware of this person's presence after we returned from our holiday travels in Texas. This person is assertive with terribly strong opinions and comes at you from the perspective of having you all figured out. It's creepy the way this person knows us and messes with our heads like a skilled CIA interrogator.

No, we do not have a ghost. No, we did not take in a boarder. No, we do not have another crazy person squatting under our house.

This new person is our daughter, Grace, who has gone through some kind of cognitive growth spurt and is, indeed, a new person. She is showing early stages of what developmental psychology people (like my husband) call "theory of mind," which, in lay terms means she can understand 1) that other people are separate from her, and 2) they can actually think for themselves.

This is huge and complicated and makes all of our lives more interesting. As Jeff, the developmental psychologist in our house (for real) says, "This is the time when children become caring, empathetic souls. Or they become brats."

Being "people persons" ourselves, Jeff and I have enjoyed getting to know this new person. We plan on inviting her to stay as long as she likes.

Provided she can stop yelling about her spicy you-know-what.

Breeders Unite!

There is a minority group in San Francisco that receives blatant discrimination. People call us derogatory names. Storeowners and restaurant staff look down their noses at us, and even refuse to serve us. We are often told that our kind isn't welcome here.

No, we are not an ethnic or religious minority. We are not a group that identifies by gender or sexual orientation.

We are parents with children. And in this tolerant and diverse and open-minded city, we are often treated like dog poop. Actually, since dogs outnumber children by ten to one in San Francisco, and the dog lobby often accomplishes more than the public school lobby, dog poop often receives higher elevation than human children.

I toyed with writing about this particular bitch of mine for months, and I almost blew the whole thing off until I went out for a drink with my friend Kim at our neighborhood martini bar, and she recounted a recent incident that set her blood aflame.

While shopping at a certain upscale wine shop, on a certain main street in Noe Valley, Kim got an earful of the kind of discrimination I'm talking about. Mr. Wine Clerk behind the counter told Kim, with utmost sincerity, that:

"We should let dogs come in the store and make parents tie their kids to the parking meters outside."

Kim, who had her two-year-old safely tucked away in the stroller, was appalled.

And so was I. I couldn't believe that any place in Noe Valley, one of San Francisco's few kid havens, would be so stupid as to thwart potential business from parents.

We were also appalled because this was not an isolated incident, even in Noe Valley, but merely an example of the type of unfriendly treatment that parents get every day.

Of course we all know about the major problems that make it hard for families in San Francisco: housing costs that assume everyone struck it rich via Google or else cashed in when a great aunt kicked the bucket; private schools that require you to spend twenty grand of that inheritance for a semester's tuition; struggling public schools with declining enrollments; unsafe public parks full of syringes and broken glass.

But beyond these big-time problems, families also find San Francisco to be unwelcoming in small, subtle (and not so subtle) ways, like in the hostile comments from wine store guys.

Around here, people without kids call us "Breeders." This name is not meant as a compliment. I wouldn't go as far as comparing the Breeder label to an ethnic slur, but it has the same intent of tearing down and demeaning its recipient.

I can anticipate the backlash of all my whining now:

"If it's so bad here, why don't you move somewhere else?"

"This is the way it is here. Deal with it or get out!"

"Breeders aren't discriminated against in the Red States, so why don't you go there!"

The irony is that many of us Breeders still love our wonderful, unique "San Francisco Values," and we think this is still a great place to raise kids. Where else could we expose our offspring to such vibrant, passionate people? We want to stay here and raise little open-minded individuals who will grow up to fearlessly embrace all kinds of diversity.

So why should a hip, funny, sophisticated, cultured, intelligent, urban person (not that I profess to be any of those things, but I know quite a few Breeders who are) suddenly become a second-class citizen just because he or she has a family? And why are kids often perceived as less deserving than dogs in our fair city?

Just like I can't convince my small daughter that stripes and plaids sometimes clash, I may not be able to convince all the Haters that we Breeders are people too. But I can say without a doubt that my family's money goes to the restaurant where the server greets my offspring with a smile, and to the wine store where I am not asked to tie my child to the parking meter outside.

An Open Letter to Justin Timberlake

Dear Justin,

Hi! How are you, Justin? I'm doing well. Work and family are keeping me busy, although I must admit that things haven't been the same since you released *FutureSex/LoveSounds*.

Because honestly, Justin, there is something I need to get off my chest: I happen to have a crush on you. There, I feel better just having said it. Does that ever happen to you, Justin? Do you ever just need to unload?

This crush has a deleterious side effect. It makes me feel old. Old like I thought of my mom as being old when I was 12 and she got all flushed and giddy when Tom Cruise slid across the hardwoods in his tighty-whiteys in *Risky Business*. Not wrinkled-neck old, but somehow less young.

I used to feel embarrassed for Mom's girlish reaction to the pre-cukoo-Cruise. I wanted to yell, "Mooo-om! Don't you even know what this movie is about? High school kids hiring hookers for a business class project! Ew! Gross!" In fact, I think I did yell that at my Mom. I was 12, after all.

But back to you, Justin. Now that I am a mom myself, I suddenly find one more reason that I empathize with my own mother. This reason is you, Justin. I now understand her bizarre, almost-maternal crush on a younger man. I suddenly understand Mom's need to yell, "Isn't he adorable!" every time we stumble across a re-run of *Cocktail* on TBS.

Like, for instance, a few months ago, when you were hosting *Saturday Night Live,* I found myself sitting through several excruciating minutes of un-funny sketch comedy just to get to your Robin Gibb impression. And this is not just because I am a number one Bee Gees super-fan who can reenact every dance sequence from *Saturday Night Fever*. It is because I wanted to see you in those tight white pants, Justin.

By the time you actually performed your own song and dance bit, I swear to God I actually thought, "That boy Justin has really got something! He's very charismatic!" And don't even get me started on the You-Know-What in a Box digital short. Even with the Chess King costume, I had to go take a cold shower.

See how old I am? I might as well have just pinched your cheek and given you a dollar.

Justin, I apologize for taking so long to hitch myself to the Timberlake bandwagon. I'm afraid I shunned N'Sync in their heyday, being too close in age (early 20s) to the boy band phenom. I spent those years trying to distance myself from bubblegum, cheesy choreography, focusing instead on too-cool, and sadly less attractive, bands like Phish and the Smashing Pumpkins.

My friend Holly also made the astute observation that we probably couldn't fully, openly appreciate hunky teen idols when we were around that age. You guys were too close to the hottie, unattainable boyfriends we never got. Now that we are older, with a few notches in our belts, we can safely pine after you and your brethren as older ladies admiring a fine male specimen. How very *Sex in the City* of us!

I thought I was alone in my newfound old-woman admiration and respect for you, Justin. Then I got a dishy email from another thirty-something mama friend of mine, confessing her unabashed desire to have you sing *Sexyback* to her in a private one-woman audience.

It made me wonder, how many other aging Gen X moms have a secret (or not so secret) fetish for you, Justin? How many other women are re-living their mothers' 1980s Tom Cruise or Rob Lowe cradle-robbing fantasies?

To be honest with you, Justin, I admit that I am less than familiar with your music and acting, honing instead a refined admiration for your other talents and skills. But I promise that as soon as I get over gazing at your hiney, I will play catch-up, beginning with that recent tune where you sing in a darling falsetto about walking on the beach with a special lady.

Justin, we have lots of nice beaches here in San Francisco, provided you wear a parka. And I understand you hold a place in your heart for women of a certain maturity level, based on your former relationship with Ms. Diaz.

Justin, I'll have you know that I am happily in love with my husband and I would never to do anything to hurt our marriage. In fact, I told my husband about our little imaginary flirtation and he is very supportive of all my creative pursuits. What did he ask for in return? No, not time with Angelina Jolie, but a mere five minutes of peace when he gets home from work every day.

Even though Jeff is going to give me a pass, I imagine you have legions of hot young women throwing their very tiny underthings at you at every show. And, based on casual observation of thongs hanging out of jeans and pre-teen lingerie departments, these underthings are much tinier than the underthings of my youthful heyday.

I know that my old-lady crush is just that, an old-lady crush. However, if you are ever in the neighborhood, look me up.

I would love to show you my first-edition Bee Gees cassettes.

Finding Out

I didn't want to find out. (Or so I thought.) I didn't find out ahead of time with the first one.

"I don't want to find out!" I shouted from the bathroom, after my hundredth visit for the evening. "Do we really have to find out?" I whined on the way to the ultrasound appointment.

Yes, that's right! It's an ultrasound appointment! I've been crossing my fingers and thanking my lucky stars about every ten seconds because we're pregnant! Finally, my wish, my hope, my dream! After a year of heartache and loss, we are at last expecting again! And now, as I celebrate the joy of everything going well for this pregnancy, I find myself reacting to a dilemma that I am grateful to have been forced to confront.

Call me old-timey, but, in this high-tech world, I like the notion of not giving away the big moment until the last minute. Just like millions of women have done before me throughout history. I find a solid, universal comfort in the climactic experience shared by families throughout time and across cultures.

But my daughter needed to know. And that became the official excuse.

She had to find out if our new baby will be a boy or a girl.

We copied the actions of a friend and decided not to find out at the actual appointment. Instead, we had the ultrasound technician write it down on a piece of paper and put it in an envelope. That way we could open it together at home, as a family.

The reactions were dramatic.

As soon as we pulled out the yellow sticky note, we handed it over to Grace, dragging out the anticipation as our four-year-old pointed out the letters. "I see an I and a T and an S and an A." She looked up expectantly, waiting to see the sex represented by her proud pronouncement.

"Keep going!" My husband, Jeff, and I both yelled.

"And I see a G," she went on.

"A GIRL!!!" we screeched again.

"I knew I was right!" Grace cried. "I was right! I was right! I knew it was a girl!" She bounced on the sofa in perfect big sister glee.

Jeff immediately punched one fist into an open palm several times in a mock protective daddy stance. "Gotta keep the boys away," he muttered. "Gotta keep those stinkin' boys away."

As for me, I laughed and cheered and shouted, "YAY!" while masking a flurry of internal reactions covering everything from relief at dodging the whole circumcision issue to thoughts about sister bonding to cutesy visions of a shared bedroom with fun matching comforters. And in our miniscule San Francisco house, the option of siblings sharing a bedroom is no small benefit.

Later at dinner, Jeff continued his old-school daddy diatribe. "Good grief!" He dropped his fork dramatically. "I'm going to have to pay for two weddings!"

"Don't worry," I said. "By the time these girls are old enough, weddings will be obsolete."

Grace, overhearing our conversation, threw in her two cents with (San Francisco Moment Alert!), "Yeah! And besides, I may marry a girl!"

"Yes, you may." Jeff and I both solemnly agreed.

This conversation and our varied family responses throughout the day led me to reflect on the whole gender identification issue. As a former women's studies student and a card-carrying, whatever-wave feminist, this is something I do a little too often.

I thought about a chat with some pregnant mommies in my prenatal yoga class, where we all discussed the pros and cons of finding out. I mentioned that we didn't find out with our first baby.

A first-time mama looked at me with wide, incredulous eyes. "Then how did you know how to decorate your nursery?"

I stared back and smiled nervously, not knowing where to start. Should I tell her about our kid not really needing her own room until she was almost one? Should I tell her about my perpetual annoyance at gender-based marketing that convinces well-meaning parents that newborns actually care if they are wearing pink or blue?

And don't even get me started on my crunchy, back-to-basics, psuedo-simplicity philosophy that thinks dropping a few grand to decorate a nursery is antithetical to my family's entire life and lifestyle—even while I appreciate the aesthetic pleasure of creating a soothing space for adults or children.

I stammered something about the small apartment we lived in when our first daughter was born. I didn't want to get into it about being too poor (by San Francisco standards) to have a nursery even if I wanted one. Especially not to the stranger with the Prada yoga tote who probably waddled in from a $1 million Victorian.

I smiled again, this time with confidence. I felt fine with my simple answer to the first-time Prada mama.

I realize that finding out the baby's sex pushed me to find out a few other things about myself as a parent. This time around I feel more certain and calm. I feel less afraid, even when daring to attempt a natural birth after a c-section. I feel more at peace, even after a series of heartbreaking miscarriages that led us to this point. I feel bolder about looking a stranger in the eye and admitting that, no, I do not have a nursery. And I feel non-judgmental if that mama tells me she does.

I feel comfortable about finding out the sex of the baby because I can handle it either way.

Sometimes it's good to find out.

And besides, sometimes these things can be wrong. In which case my son will have a delightful pink wardrobe he will inherit from his big sister.

Epilogue

Well, she came out fine and she was still a girl.

Rosemary Lilah was born shortly after I finished the draft of this book. She shot out of me like a pink bullet, blazing in a new era for our family. Suddenly, our house felt smaller, my time-worn patience stretched thinner, and my family in Texas felt further and further away. It is too soon at this time to accurately quantify the long-term effects of doubling the number of children in our house, but I can tell you that having two babies doubles the tension of the ongoing tug-of-war between Texas and San Francisco. My heart still wrestles with wanting to raise the girls back "home" and wanting to expose them to the thrills of the City for as long as possible.

The addition of Rosemary has resurrected all of the urban struggles associated with babyhood: wrestling with strollers on public transportation, trying to find a parking spot while an infant screeches for twenty blocks, and finding a sense of home in a city that is often downright hostile to babies and children. I am also reunited with the joy of walking my baby over scenic hills with breathtaking views of the Bridges and the Bay, the satisfaction of carrying my infant in a sling through a crowded farmers' market that brims with tasty California produce, and the sense of vibrant, diverse community I feel taking my children to school, to church, or to any number of crowded playgrounds.

Fortunately, San Francisco parenting, with all of its conflicting flavors, continues to provide a wealth of material for my creative pursuits. Before Rosemary was born, I liked to tell Jeff that we could never move because I need Grace tearing around the city for writing material. It's thrilling to now have twice the inspiration.

Look for Rosemary to star in the next book.

Acknowledgements

Thank you to my writer friends.

Thank you, Linda Sharp, for the complimentary (and complementary) editing of this book, and for first publishing many of these essays on your website, *Sanity Central.* Linda, you earn your name with your sharp editing skills and even sharper wit.

Thank you, Karrie McAllister, my friend across cyberspace. You live on the other side of the looking glass where your *Small Town Soup* stories mirror my weirdo city-mommy stories in strange and familiar ways.

Thank you to my neighborhood paper, *The Noe Valley Voice,* for originally printing several of these essays.

Thank you to *Mothering* magazine for originally printing "It's a Sling Thing," as "The Magic Cloth."

Thank you, Writing Group (aka "Talking Group") Jill Wesley, Holly Hirsh, and Sue Morosoli. You always offer constructive feedback, consistent laughs, and true friendship. You ladies continue to surprise and impress me.

Thank you, Kim Girard, for the support of a "real" writer. You give tough criticism when I need it and kind words when I'm too tender for the harsh stuff.

Thank you to indie-published mommy-zines, *Fertile Ground, Bad Mother Chronicles, The Imperfect Parent,* and *Mamazine* for originally printing several of these essays. Thanks to many other awesome mommy-zines including *Mamaphiles, Lone Star Ma, Gemini, Tenderfoot, The East Village Inky, Hip Mama,* and many others for the creative inspiration.

Thank you to my family.

Thank you, Naomi Ingram, my grandma who loyally reads every word I write, no matter how dull or vulgar.

Thank you, Mary Dutton, my grandma who inspired me to be a writer when I first read your best-selling novel, *Thorpe*, at age 13. (And then cried all afternoon because it was so good!)

Thank you, Lara Weber, for the free cover art, for being the best little sister ever, and for being a fool.

Thanks, Mom and Dad, for the computer that year for Christmas. Oh, and for everything else.

Thanks, Grace and Rosemary for all of the fodder. I hope I can continue this until you are teenagers and you get too embarrassed.

Thank you, Jeff. You may be portrayed as a goofball in my writing but you know that you are my best friend and the love of my life. Thank you for always supporting my dreams.

About the Author

Robin Dutton-Cookston's writing can be found in many print and web publications, including *Mothering, Hip Mama, Clamor, Mamaphiles,* and *Mom Writers Literary Magazine.* She is senior editor at *Mom Writer's Literary Magazine* and a regular contributor to *The Noe Valley Voice.* She also puts out an old-fashioned photocopied zine called *Apron Strings: A Zine for Mamas, Papas, and People Who Have Them,* whenever the mood strikes and time permits. In addition to her creative writing pursuits, Robin works for San Francisco's official website for families, www.SFkids.org. Please visit *The Foggiest Idea* website at www.thefoggiestidea.wordpress.com.

Printed in the United States
131196LV00005B/223-243/P